Keto Diet Cookbook For Beginners

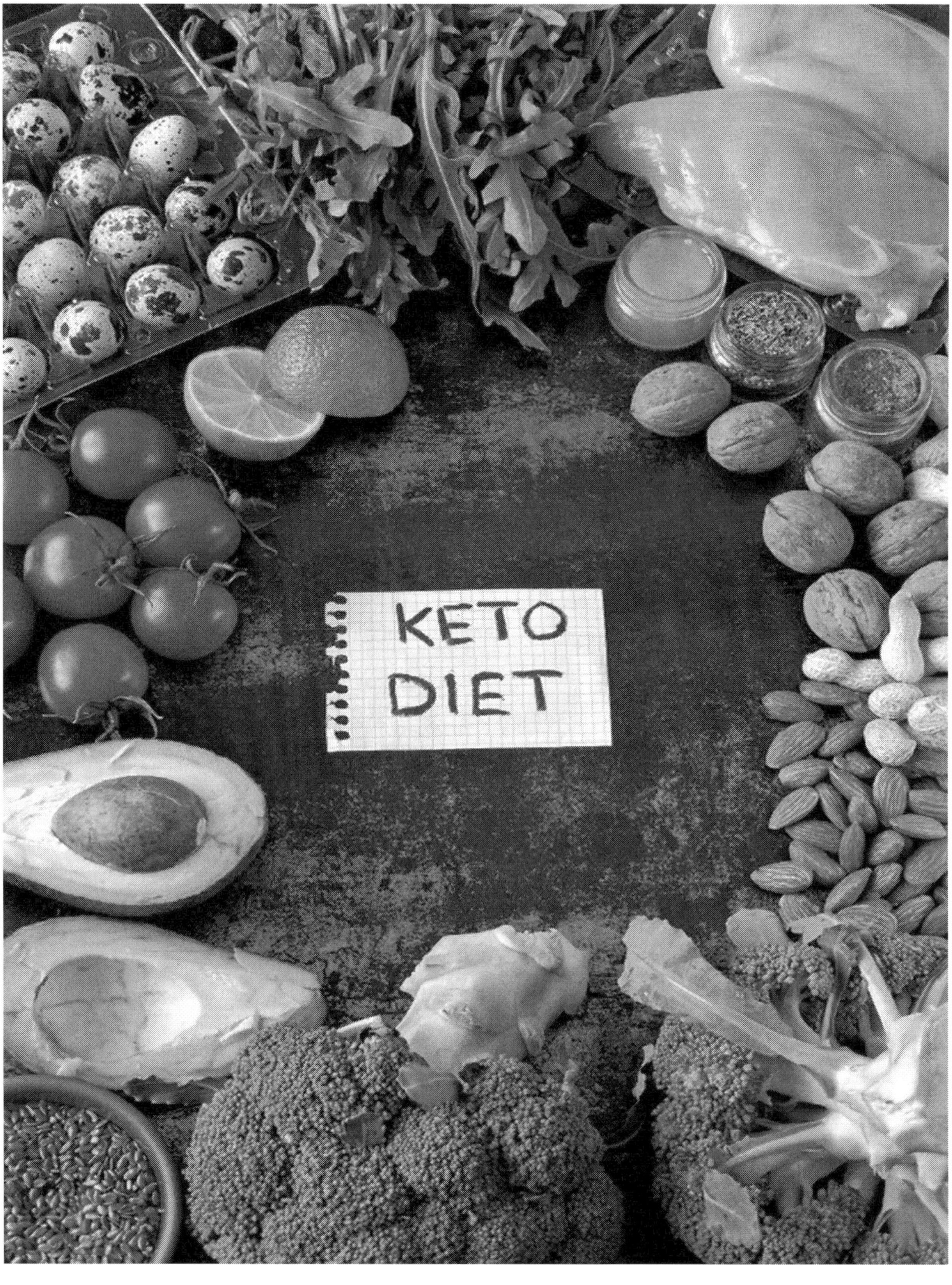
KETO
DIET

Keto Diet Cookbook For Beginners

The Keto diet basic principles and easy-to-cook delicious recipes-This keto diet cookbook make following a low-carb, high-fat diet so much easier.

Aliza Silva

Copyright@2020 by Published in the United States by Aliza Silva

All Rights Reserved.

No part of this publication or the information in it may be quoted from or reproduced in any form by means such as printing, scanning, photocopying or otherwise without prior written permission of the copyright holder.

Disclaimer and Terms of Use:

Consistent efforts have been made to make sure that the information provided in this book is accurate and complete. However, the author or publisher doesn't guarantee the accuracy of the information, graphics, and text contained within the e-Book mainly due to the rapidly changing nature of research, science, known and unknown facts on the internet. The author and publisher are not held responsible for errors, contra interpretation or any omission regarding the subject. This e-Book is presented mainly for informational and motivational purposes only. This book is presented solely for Cooking and informational purposes only.

TABLE OF CONTENTS

INTRODUCTION 11

What is a Ketogenic Lifestyle/Diet? 12

    Understanding Carbs 12

    Why Fat is Better: 14

    Common Keto Misconceptions: 15

    Who Can and Can't Use It? 16

    Keto and Other Diets: 17

What you'll Eat And What you ought to Avoid 20

    Food to Eat: 20

        Meat/seafood: 20

        Vegetables/fruit: 21

        Nuts/seeds (in moderation): 21

        Full-fat dairy: 22

        Fats/oils: 22

        Beverages: 22

        Baking/cooking supplies: 22

    Foods to avoid: 23

        Processed meats: 23

        Grain: 23

        High-carb veggies and fruit: 23

        Low-fat or fat-free dairy: 24

        Beans/legumes: 24

        Certain oils: 24

        Refined + artificial sweeteners: 24

        Other: 25

Benefits of the Ketogenic Diet 25

    Cutting out lots of carbs can lead to weight loss 25

    The diet improves energy levels 25

Your skin and hair health improve 26

The keto diet might prevent certain diseases 26

TIPS TO HELP YOU LIVE A HAPPIER KETO LIFESTYLE 26

Make Yours! 26

Counting your macros is essential! 27

Ditch those carb-rich foods before you start 27

Treat yourself! 27

Greens! Greens! Greens! 28

Get organized 28

Drink plenty of water & Exercise 28

Make sense of eating out 28

MY WEIGHT LOSS TIPS WITH KETO 29

Until Keto! 29

I faced my issues 29

I didn't quit 29

I retrained my eating habits 30

I planned my meals 30

I kept a food diary 30

I stayed flexible 30

I focused on me 31

How about me? 31

Keto FAQs 32

How can I know that I am in ketosis? 32

How should I track my ketone level? 32

How ketosis work in my body? 32

Is a keto diet being safe for diabetic people? 32

Can I eat fruits during keto diet? 32

How long it takes to get me into ketosis? 32

SMOOTHIES & BREAKFAST 33

- Breakfast Blueberry Coconut Smoothie 34
- BLUEBERRY SMOOTHIE: 35
- Morning Berry-Green Smoothie: 36
- Strawberry Smoothie: 37
- Super food Red Smoothie: 38
- GREEN KETO SMOOTHIE: 39
- Bacon and Cheese Frittata: 40
- Blueberry Bread: 41
- Creamy Vanilla Keto Cappuccino: 42
- KETO CHEESE OMELET: 43
- Ham & Egg Broccoli Bake: 44
- Bacon Omelet: 45
- Yummy Blue Cheese & Mushroom Omelet: 46

POULTRY 47
- Rosemary Chicken with Avocado Sauce: 48
- FRIED MARINATED CHICKEN: 49
- Spinach Chicken Cheesy Bake: 50
- Roasted Whole Chicken: 51
- Green Bean & Broccoli Chicken Stir-Fry: 52
- BUFFALO CHICKEN PIZZA: 53
- Spinach & Ricotta Stuffed Chicken Breasts: 54
- Tangy Chicken Breasts: 55
- Hot Chicken Meatballs: 56
- KETO CHICKEN ENCHILADAS: 57
- Spicy Chicken Leg Quarters: 58
- Stuffed Avocados with Chicken: 59
- KETO GLUTEN-FREE CHICKEN AND DUMPLINGS: 60

BEEF & LAMB 61
- Asian Spiced Beef with Broccoli: 62

KETO BEEF LASAGNA: 63

Italian Beef Ragout: 64

Cocktail Chili Beef Meatballs: 65

KETO INSTANT POT BEEF STEW: 66

Beef with Dilled Yogurt: 67

Lamb Curry: 68

Lamb Kebabs with Mint Yogurt: 69

GRILLED CHERMOULA LAMB CHOPS: 70

North African Lamb: 71

Broiled Lamb Chops: 72

Stuffed Lamb Shoulder: 73

LAMB SLIDERS: 74

PORK **75**

Barbecued Pork Chops: 76

Pork Sausage Bake: 77

Pork Stroganoff: 78

Baked Pork Sausage with Vegetables: 79

Pork Osso Bucco: 80

Fried Pork & Cilantro: 81

Pork Steaks with Carrot & Broccoli: 82

Pork Nachos: 83

Pork with Brussels Sprout: 84

Roasted Pork Stuffed with Ham & Cheese: 85

Garlicky Pork with Bell Peppers: 86

Pork Liver with Scallion: 87

Mushroom Pork Chops with Steamed Broccoli: 88

FISH & SEAFOOD **89**

Crispy Salmon with Broccoli & Red Bell Pepper: 90

SHRIMP AND BLACK BEAN ENCHILADAS: 91

Tuna Steaks with Shirataki Noodles: 92
Cod in Butter Sauce: 93
Sardines with Green Pasta & Sun-Dried Tomatoes: 94
TILAPIA WITH PARMESAN BARK: 95
Blackened Fish Tacos with Slaw: 96
Parmesan Halibut: 97
Fish Tacos with Slaw, Lemon and Cilantro: 98
MOZZARELLA FISH: 99
Sushi Shrimp Rolls: 100
Lemony Trout: 101
Prawns in Creamy Mushroom Sauce: 102

VEGGIES & SIDES **103**
Tofu & Vegetable Stir-Fry: 104
KETO PEANUT BUTTER RAMEN: 105
Cauliflower Gouda Casserole: 106
Cabbage Casserole: 107
Mediterranean Eggplant Squash Pasta: 108
SIMPLE VEGAN BOK CHOY SOUP: 109
Creamy Vegetable Stew: 110
Broccoli Mash: 111
Roasted Brussels Sprouts & Bacon: 112
KETO CAULIFLOWER HASH BROWNS: 113
Zucchini Gratin with Feta Cheese: 114
Spiced mushroom: 115
Roasted Green Beans with Garlic & Almond Flakes: 116

DESSERTS & DRINKS **117**
Coconut Panna Cotta with Cream & Caramel: 118
Chocolate Marshmallows: 119
Vanilla Crème Brûlée: 120

Healthy Chia Pudding with Strawberries: 121

Lemon Cheesecake Mousse: 122

Chocolate Lava Cake: 123

Almond Milk Berry Shake: 124

Creamy Coconut Kiwi Drink: 125

Butter Coffee: 126

Green Detox Drink: 127

Ginger Lemonade: 128

Iced Coffee: 129

CONCLUSION: **130**

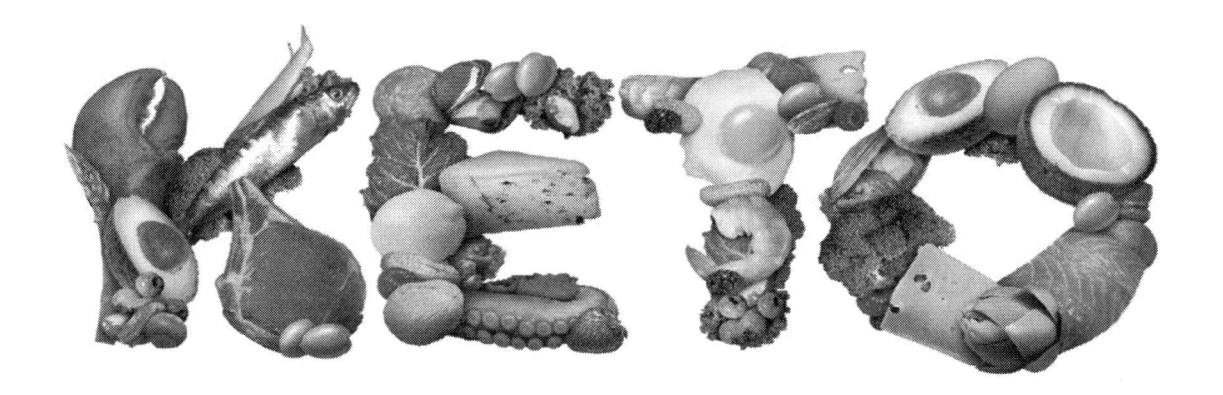

INTRODUCTION

Hello! Thanks for purchasing this book, "Keto Diet Cookbook For Beginners."

This book is for people that are considering the ketogenic diet or have decided to require it on and need to understand the knowledge on the way to start. Whether you're trying to reduce, improve your energy levels, or protect yourself against certain diseases, your diet should be working with you, not against you. The ketogenic diet is often an important pathway to healthiness.

I'm a devotee of great food and a Keto dieter. I'm not a nutritionist, professional chef, or doctor, but I even have done extensive research and cooked many keto-friendly recipes. during this book, I've collected all of the knowledge you would like to urge started, and I've done my best to word it in a way that's easy to know. The ketogenic diet has some science lingo and infrequently complicated processes related to it, but I've been bound to describe it beat a readable way. There are many scientific studies and articles online that get further into the science side of things if you're curious about learning more.

Eating well is extremely important. The ketogenic diet cuts out processed and artificial food, embraces real, high-quality ingredients, and has changed tons of people's lives. By purchasing this book, you've decided that you simply want to be one among them, so let's get started!

What is a Ketogenic Lifestyle/Diet?

To place into simple terms, the keto or ketogenic diet is a diet reliant on consuming a very low amount of carbohydrates and instead emphasizing the consumption of a high-fat diet in order to produce energy for the body. By following this diet, a user can put his or her body into a state of ketosis. In this chapter, we will go deeper into what it means to produce the body's energy in this way as opposed to other diets, as well as what a state of ketosis suggests.

Understanding Carbs

Around the world, it is not uncommon for carbohydrates to make up most or about half of a person's daily dietary consumption. If we take a moment to look at what is the standard for an American diet, in particular, regular recommendations will ask that carbohydrates comprise a percentage of as low as 45 and up to 65 percent of your total calories on a day-to-day basis (USDA, 2015). For example, if we assume you take in about 2,000 calories a day, it would mean that anywhere from 900 to 1,300 of your daily calories would derive from carbs, which would translate to anywhere from 200 up to 325 grams of carbs in a single day.

After consumption and during the digestive process, the carbohydrates will break down and become fractional portions of sugar in the forms of fructose and glucose. It is then the job of the small intestines to absorb the glucose and fructose and assist in getting them into the bloodstream, which will then carry the sugars to the liver. Once in the liver, all of these will go through a process of conversion that will convert them into glucose. It is then, with the assistance of the body's insulin, that the glucose from the liver is carried back into the bloodstream and distributed throughout the body to provide energy. This energy is used for everything from physical exertion, whether it is a walk or heavy workout, to ensure that you are breathing.

In the case that your body is not in immediate need of the glucose, the glucose will then be stored. The body stores unneeded glucose as glycogen primarily in the skeletal muscles and in the liver as well. Storing the glucose this way, the body will be able to hold onto about 2,000 calories worth of glycogen (Cathe, 2018). If the storage of glycogen reaches a point of over 2,000 calories, the body will instead begin to store the carbohydrates moving through your body as fat (Elaine K. Luo, MD, March 2017).

Glucose is made from the carbohydrates that you eat. Glucose is made possible as your pancreas produces the insulin needed to transport the glucose into your bloodstream, which then transports to your cells to use for energy in various parts of the body. This same insulin is responsible for signaling the liver and the muscle tissues that it is time to save extra glucose, as well as informing the liver when the body can no longer store more glucose.

Occasionally, the liver can have a difficult time verifying that the insulin is handled in the proper fashion and more insulin becomes needed to achieve a job. The pancreas reacts, thus creating a surge in the levels of insulin in your body to ensure that your levels of blood sugar don't become unbalanced. But rarely is this enough to secure that everything is taken care of, so excess levels of glucose often become left in your bloodstream. As a result, you experience a sudden boost of energy while eating, but end up feeling tired right after the sudden drop in energy.

None of this energy fluctuation is an issue after you have acclimated your body to the keto diet and use fat as the primary source of energy. The body becomes so efficient at burning off the extra fat that soon it will burn off the extra body fat that is hanging around the body as well.

Why Fat is Better:

Following the Standard American Diet or SAD means that the average person takes in somewhere in the ballpark of 220 grams of carbohydrates in a single day, as opposed to a ketogenic diet which restricts carb intake to an absolute maximum of 50 grams per day (USDA, 2018), and even then it only applies for those whose bodies can handle it effectively. Before long, your body will have adapted to your new diet and will become a lean, mean, fat-burning machine!

No longer will you rely on carbohydrates and glucose to fuel you. Instead, while storing all the excess away into fat where it sits unused and gathering, that store will actually be used as your body attunes to using fat as its primary energy source. The levels of blood sugar in your body will not be fluctuating via booming spikes, only to plummet moments later, but it will be able to maintain a constant and steady flow of energy, which will last you all day.

So, if you're no longer taking in a high amount of carbohydrates as a part of your daily diet, then how does all this change occur from starting a high fat, ketogenic diet? Even once your body has stopped depending on, or even being able to rely on, the consumption of carbohydrates in order to get glucose, it will still produce energy but will have to turn to the stores of fat to achieve it.

These stored fats will go to the liver: and once there, the fats will be broken down into glucose and as a byproduct of the liver with fat, the element which we call ketones, or ketone bodies is produced (Rachel Nall, RN, May 2017). The three ketones which are formed from this process are acetate, acetoacetate, and a ketone known as BHB (Perfect Keto, 2019), which is shorthand for beta-hydroxybutyrate. These ketones, once created, act as your body's primary source of energy for activating the body in what is known as a state of ketosis.

Beta-hydroxybutyrate, it ought to be noted, is not technically known as a ketone element, however, despite its chemical structure because of its role when it comes to the keto diet, it is commonly regarded as a ketone anyway. When the liver breaks down fat and ketogenesis are taking place, the first of the ketones to be produced is acetoacetate, which then forms into either BHB or acetone, though the acetone is a randomly created side effect of the acetoacetate process. Despite the simple nature of acetone, it is used to transport energy through the body, although it is used very sparsely compared to BHB. Once it is no longer needed for the body's energy, it is broken down and will be removed via urine or breathing. For this reason, acetone is what is behind the commonly noted fruity smell of someone's breath who is on the ketogenic diet. (Vladimir Stojanovic and Sherri Ihle, 2011).

Common Keto Misconceptions:

Potential dangers associated with ketosis: Assuming you discuss your particular needs with a healthcare provider and stick to the recommended guidelines, there is no reason your time spent on the keto diet shouldn't be largely risk-free. With that being said, however, there are some issues you should be aware of so that you can move forward fully aware of just what you are endeavoring.

Another potential issue accompanies the fact that the keto diet can lead to low blood sugar early on in the transition process, which means that it can be a risky proposition for those with diabetes that do not have it under control. This risk is due to the fact that carbs are a common means of helping control blood sugar levels, and many of the most common low blood sugar cures are carb-based. While there is research that suggests the diet might be relatively benign for those with type 2 diabetes, the risk of low blood sugar is still present. (Kristeen Cherney, 2017).

Additionally, for those without the willpower to maintain it, the keto diet could lead to eventual yoyo dieting. As the weight will likely come back if you change your eating habits, it can easily promote yoyo dieting which is a problem, as regaining weight may lead to other negative effects. Specifically, yoyo dieting in the long-term can lead to an increase of stubborn abdominal fat as well as an increased risk of diabetes. Generally speaking, the ability to stick to a diet is more important in the long-run than the type of diet you choose to follow. This rule means that if you are having a hard time following the keto diet, then it may not be for you.

Who Can and Can't Use It?

Generally speaking, if you are in good health and don't have any extenuating circumstances, then you can get started on the keto diet without delay. However, Pappas (2018) cautions how many individuals should speak with a primary healthcare provider before they get started to ensure they don't accidentally end up doing more harm than good, such as the following:

- Those who are already considered underweight or feel as though they might have an eating disorder.
- Anyone under 18 years of age.
- Women who are pregnant or breastfeeding.
- Anyone who is recovering from a prolonged illness or serious injury.
- Those with a history of serious mental issues.
- Those with kidney issues.
- Those who are taking medications that impair liver or kidney function.
- Women who have previously had issues with irregular periods.

- Anyone with a chronic respiratory condition.

Keto and Other Diets:

Due to the limits of the diet, it is often wrongly compared to the same as the popular Atkins diet. This misconception comes from the fact that despite some similarities, in essence, and practice, the Atkins diet is used mainly as a weight loss plan, which yields potential benefits in short-term use. Whereas the ketogenic diet is a lifestyle change, which affects the overall health of the body in various ways, as well as allows the body to engage in an entirely natural change to the metabolic use of energy.

The only overlap that tends to exists between using the keto diet and that of the Atkins diet is during the initial stages of implementation, where it is common for one who is taking on either diet to use a similar ratio of nutrients in both the keto and Atkins diet. But over even just a short amount of time, the differences between the two, especially in the ratio of nutrients that would be observably equal at the start of both diets, start to become more and more apparent.

When it comes to the ketogenic diet, you will want to watch your intake of carbs, protein, and fat closely so that you can keep an eye on your body's macros in order to maintain growth and health. Whereas the Atkins diet will allow someone on the diet to begin to introduce more carbs into their day-to-day meals after he or she has completed the first stage of the diet. Even though the Atkins diet does limit carbs and increases fats like the ketogenic diet, but in a small quantity, it still makes a huge difference when attempting to make a comparison to how it works next to the keto diet.

When it comes to the keto diet, on a day-to-day basis, up to 70 or 80 percent of your consumed calories will be coming from healthy fat foods (Julia Malacoff, 2018) to make sure that your body is going through the process of producing ketones and then using those ketones as the primary source of energy for the body and brain. Though results that occur initially due to the Atkins diet are very effective at the outset, they will not last over an extended period of time. Someone who is on the keto diet, on the other hand, will not only experience weight loss at the beginning of his or her journey but will be able to easily maintain both the loss of weight, as well as all the other health benefits that accompany the diet.

People are also seen when looking over the option of the keto diet and lifestyle to give it the same eye as the Paleo or Paleolithic diet. In the case of these two, when placing into a dietary arena for closer study, there is at least a lot more than the two have in common with one another, as opposed to comparing a keto and Atkins diet. Because these comparisons do not aid in quelling the confusion about the two, we are going to take some time to cover both what is similar between the keto and paleo diet before getting into just what makes each one unique.

The first of the similarities between the two is in focus on the quality of food that each diet has you consuming. Though within each person's budgetary limits, it is true for both the keto and paleo diets that real, whole, and high-quality food is a recommendation over foods that are refined and contain excessive additives.

If you are someone who enjoys seafood which is a healthy meal as a part of both diets, it is best to be able to get fish that is caught in the wild like salmon rather than anything that is farm-raised. The same applies to any meats that you will be consuming on either diet. It is preferred that the meat you buy and eat is grass-fed. Animals that are eating grass out in the open may not grow as big as ones that are fed corn with additives, but the meat that comes as a result of how they eat is much healthier for you and contains more nutrients.

The higher quality of the grass-fed animals also needs to be taken into account when it comes to looking at dairy products. Butter that comes from an animal that is grass-fed is encouraged for the use of cooking, as well as coconut oil and olive oil. There are harmful fats that are commonly used for cooking that you will want to avoid such as canola oil and corn.

In both diets as well, you will be either severely reducing or eliminating altogether the consumption of refined grains and legumes. When it comes to the paleo diet, the aim is to mimic the diet of our early human ancestors. It is the case both for many grains and for legumes that they were in fact not a common part of the diets for early humans. These legumes and grains causing digestive issues are due to the practice of the cultivation of crops not taking place until around 10,000 years ago.

As far as the keto diet, it is not a bad idea to avoid legumes altogether. They have within them a compound which is known as an anti-nutrient. The anti-nutrients contained within them include phytates and lectins, (Jaclyn Tolentino, 2019) both of which can interfere with your process of digestion. When it comes to the Paleolithic diet, sugar is avoided outright because it is considered to be a processed food. Despite this restriction, however, unlike the ketogenic diet, it is not uncommon for a paleo diet to allow for such things as honey and maple syrup.

When on the keto diet and eliminating or restricting the three of these things — sugar, legumes, and grains, it is necessary for the overall health effects of all three as well as their carbohydrates. The consumption of any of these has caused issues with inflammation, spikes in levels of blood sugar, and a resistance to insulin. And in regards to trying to maintain a keto diet and remain in ketosis, these foods work against those issues due to the high carbohydrates contained. The final similarity between both the keto and the paleo diet is that either one could technically be used in order to reach a health goal, which resembles results from the other.

In both the paleo diet as well as the keto diet, weight loss is a common occurrence. Both are allegedly more reliable as tools for losing weight, rather than just restricting the calories that one eats. And, of course, for both, the loss of weight seems to only be the beginning.

When it comes to comparing the two, they start to really split off when examining the long-term results due to the difference in the focus of each diet. On the one hand, on the ketogenic diet, you do so because you intend to get your body into the metabolic state of ketosis, which will only be done through the consumption of a certain amount of macronutrients, which means the limiting of carbohydrates. The idea is to be able to get your body away from using carbohydrates as its source of energy and focus it on the gear of using fat as fuel.

The distinction between keto and paleo when it comes to intentionality is that the paleo diet is focused simply on eating a diet, which is similar to that of our ancestors. Thus, it offers the benefit of eliminating particular foods in the average diet which are largely considered to have a negative effect on health. Instead, it and places more of a focus on the consumption of foods that are organic and whole, so it is a byproduct of chance. The intention of the diet is on health, yes, but it is not necessarily a low carbohydrate diet and does not induce a metabolic change in the body.

Because the paleo diet is not one which intends to be low in carb intake, its effects result as quite different from that of the keto diet. Though the reducing on the consumption of sugar, grains, and legumes in the paleo diet may unintentionally have the effect of lowering the number of carbs you are eating, because it is not the focus of the diet, you will still generally end up eating plenty of carbs in the forms of high carb fruits, honey, and sweet potatoes. Because of this transition, your body will still be relying on the use of glucose for its energy.

The keto diet, however, is far more restrictive, cutting down even on the fruits and vegetables that you are recommended to eat. When it comes to the ketogenic diet as well, there is some allowance for dairy products. The paleo diet, due to the lack of dairy which was available for early humans, eliminated dairy altogether and outright. On the other hand, the keto diet will allow for a moderate amount of dairy products that are high in quality for people who are able to hand consuming them. If it does not cause any discomfort in the consumer, the ketogenic diet allows someone who is on it to eat raw milk, cheese, and even sour cream.

What you'll Eat And What you ought to Avoid

For being a restrictive diet, the list of foods you can eat is relatively extensive. All kinds of meat and seafood (ideally grass-fed, wild-caught, and organic) are allowed, while all full-fat dairy is also encouraged. You can eat lots of low-carb vegetables, as well, though you're more limited on fruit. A banana every now and then shouldn't throw you out of ketosis, however, but you should always be careful about what else you eat that day. Here's a fairly complete list of everything

Food to Eat:

Meat/seafood:

Beef (ideally grass-fed)
Eggs (ideally cage-free and organic)
Fish/shellfish (ideally wild-caught)
Goat
Lamb

Organ meats
Pork (ideally free-range and organic)
Poultry (organic)

Vegetables/fruit:

Alfalfa sprouts
Avocado
Berries (blackberries, raspberries, cranberries, etc)
Bell peppers
Bok choy
Broccoli
Button mushrooms
Cabbage
Cauliflower
Celery
Citrus (lemons, oranges, limes)
Cucumber
Eggplant
Garlic
Kale
Lettuce
Onions
Parsley
Radishes
Sea vegetables
Spinach
Swiss chard
Tomatoes
Watercress
Zucchini

Nuts/seeds (in moderation):

Almonds
Brazil nuts
Chia seeds
Flax seeds
Macadamia nuts
Pecans
Pumpkin seeds
Shredded coconut (unsweetened)
Sunflower seeds
Walnuts

Full-fat dairy:

Cheese (cheddar, parmesan, mozzarella, brie, ricotta, etc)
Cottage cheese
Cream cheese
Dairy-free milk alternatives (unsweetened almond milk, coconut milk, macadamia nut milk)
Greek yogurt (plain and unsweetened)
Heavy cream

Fats/oils:

Almond oil
Avocado oil
Cocoa butter
Coconut oil/coconut cream
Duck fat
Ghee (clarified butter)
Nut butter (in moderation)
Olive oil (cold-pressed extra-virgin)

Beverages:

Sparkling water + seltzers (w/out added sweeteners)
Unsweetened coconut water
Unsweetened coffee (or sweetened with natural o-calorie sweetener)
Unsweetened herbal tea (or sweetened with natural o-calorie sweetener)
Water

Baking/cooking supplies:

Almond flour
Baking powder/baking soda (aluminum-free)
Coconut aminos (soy sauce substitute)
Coconut flour
Erythritol/stevia blends
Fish sauce
Mayonnaise (w/out added sugar)
Monk fruit extract or powder
Psyllium husk (a thickener)
Spices + herbs
Sugar-free ketchup
Sugar-free yellow mustard
Vinegar (white, wine, and apple cider)

Xanthan gum (in very small amounts)

Foods to avoid:

Knowing what to avoid on the ketogenic diet is determined by asking yourself two questions: Is it low-carb? Does it have artificial ingredients? Foods too high in carbs will throw you out of ketosis when you eat too much, while anything with artificial or processed ingredients also tends to be too high in carbs, while also being just unhealthy. Here's what to avoid:

Processed meats:

Deli meat
Grain-fed meats
Hot dogs
Sausages

Grain:

Barley
Buckwheat
Corn
Oatmeal
Quinoa
Rice
Wheat
Wheat gluten

High-carb veggies and fruit:

Artichokes
Bananas
Carrots
Clementines
Dried fruit
Fruit syrups
Grapes
Jam/jelly
Kiwi
Mangos
Pears

Pineapple
Potatoes
Squash
Sweet potatoes
Watermelon
Yams

Low-fat or fat-free dairy:

Fake butter alternatives
Low-fat/fat-free cream cheese
Low-fat/fat-free sour cream
Low-fat/fat-free yogurt
Skim milk

Beans/legumes:

Black
Chickpeas
Fava
Kidney
Lentils
Peas
White

Certain oils:

Canola
Corn
Grapeseed
Peanut
Sesame
Soybean
Sunflower

Refined + artificial sweeteners:

Agave
Aspartame
Cane sugar
Coconut sugar
Corn syrup
Equal

Honey
Maple syrup
Raw sugar
Saccharin
Splenda
Sucralose
White sugar

Other:

Alcohol
Baked goods + treats
Diet foods
Fast food

Benefits of the Ketogenic Diet

Why are people going on the ketogenic diet even if they don't have epilepsy? As the keto diet became a more popular alternative to fasting, people began noticing additional benefits, like weight loss. Here are the most reported benefits of the low-carb, high-fat diet:

Cutting out lots of carbs can lead to weight loss

Significantly restricting carbs causes the body to produce ketones, but it also prevents excess glucose from getting stored as body fat. Lots of people who go on the keto diet find that losing weight is much easier. This is very true if your current diet is high in refined, simple carbs like light bread, pasta, and sugar. Carbs are not inherently evil - as we mentioned before, the body actually needs them - but refined carbs are not very nutritious and usually end up stored as fat. When you eliminate them, weight loss is more likely.

The diet improves energy levels

You probably are familiar with the sluggish feeling after eating a carb-heavy meal. That's because your body is working so hard to process the carbs. You get an initial burst of energy and then a crash. When you cut out those refined carbs and instead eat foods higher in fat, that fatigue goes away. Your blood sugar levels become more stabilized throughout the day instead of going on a rollercoaster. The high-fat diet also helps with mental energy, since the brain is especially fond of fats found in coconut oil and fatty fish.

Your skin and hair health improve

A lot of individuals who continue the keto diet report having healthier skin, hair, and even fingernails. Fat is a hydrating nutrient, and hair and skin love it. Hair becomes shinier, sleeker, and less brittle. Skin also becomes healthier and less dry, while cutting out inflammatory foods like sugar can help clear up acne.

The keto diet might prevent certain diseases

There isn't plenty of research into the keto diet's effect on disease, but early studies are intriguing. Heart disease is a top killer, especially in the United States, and the keto diet can help people maintain better blood pressure. A high body mass is linked to heart disease, so losing weight thanks to the keto diet can also protect a person from the disease. The keto diet's effect on the brain is also significant, and studies have shown that ketones might help prevent and even treat brain disorders like Alzheimer's.

TIPS TO HELP YOU LIVE A HAPPIER KETO LIFESTYLE

Don't you wish that someone would just hand you a list of Keto lifestyle hacks that would help you get to grips and lose weight, gain energy, and feel terrific faster?

Well, today's your lucky day because that's what I've just done for you.

Make Yours!
I feel like a full flute of champagne with an attitude saying this; you've got to make yours!

When you start a Keto diet, it often seems like an easy thing to get the carbs of the menu. Just skip the bread, pasta, potatoes, and rice, and you're done! It isn't that simple; I'm afraid to say. Carbs and more specifically, sugars are in almost every processed food you buy from yogurts to condiments, sauces, and much more in between.

The best way to beat these carbs is to merely avoid these foods entirely and make your versions. Not only can you control the carbs like this, but you can also tweak the recipe, so it's exactly how you love your food to be. If you absolutely must eat processed food, check your labels!

Counting your macros is essential!

I'm a laid-back kind of person, and I like to think that once I've understood a concept, I can go ahead without worrying about the details. However, you can't do this when it comes to Keto. As unusual as it might seem, you absolutely must count your macros - your net carb, protein, and fat intake.

Ditch those carb-rich foods before you start

There's nothing worse than feeling like you're comfortable on the Keto diet and super-happy with your progress, only to find a packet of potato chips or long-forgotten cheese fries lurking at the back of the pantry. Bang! There goes your willpower! Even if you have firm resolve, it's quite likely you'll succumb to temptation.

Avoid this problem by thoroughly cleaning your pantry before you get started with Keto.

I understand that if you have a partner or family members around who aren't following the Keto diet, this can be a hard task. In this case, I suggest you grab a large box, place their high-carb foods inside and keep it out of sight!

If you're the one doing the family cooking, a lot of discipline is needed not to have a bite of those pasta dishes when you make them. Let the others do the taste checks when you cook.

Treat yourself!

Just because you're going Keto, doesn't mean you should start eating horrible stodgy foods. Don't follow such boring websites that show these; Keto can be fun-loving. This isn't about eating trash. It's about nourishing your body with exactly what it needs, and that includes your taste buds too.

You absolutely can continue eating like a foodie and enjoy those tender gnocchi in marinara sauce, or fragrant Nasi goreng, or fantastically spiced Indian Lamb Curry. That's exactly why I've written this book; there's a way to go about it.

Greens! Greens! Greens!

It's vital that you eat plenty of green leafy veggies while you're on Keto. They are one of the planet's best sources of minerals and add more fiber, antioxidants and even protein to your healthy diet. I love kale, spring greens, and spinach, but any will do.

Don't be afraid to include plenty of other low carb veggies too. Provided you keep your eye on your macros, they make a very nourishing, healthy addition to your diet that will keep your heart healthy, help prevent cancer and boost your digestive system too.

Get organized

The Organization is key to simplifying your Keto lifestyle, which helps you to stick to the diet. Plan your meals at the start of the week, organize a grocery list and go shopping ideally once to save you some time and energy.

It's also a good idea to cook extra portions of food at once while cooking. Most of the recipes in this book work excellently (and often taste better!) when made in advance. Use your fridge and freezer to store the leftovers, and you'll only have to reheat.

Drink plenty of water & Exercise

As well as eating the right foods, it's also important to stay hydrated. Get a refillable water bottle, fill it up and carry it with you. Aim for a minimum of 2 liters of water per day. Staying active with stressless exercises helps your body get into Ketosis and burns more fat while being excellent for your entire body, mind, and spirit.

Nevertheless, remember, it will take a couple of weeks for your body to adjust to the Keto lifestyle to start seeing the weight loss results you hope for, so don't go too hard on yourself. Slow and steady exercises do the trick.

Make sense of eating out

There's nothing worse than being 'that person' who can't eat a thing on the menu at a restaurant. So, do your homework!

Before you go anywhere, check out your local restaurants and find out if there's anything on the menu that will suit you. Check out the restaurants' online menus or pick up the phone and give them a call.

It is fantastic to find your perfect restaurant; once you do, visit them often for your comfort.

Got it? Awesome! There's just one last topic I'd like to cover before we move forward to the recipes, and that's weight loss. Yes, I know I've talked about it plenty of times already, but it does deserve some space. Because, dare I say it, changing your eating habits isn't enough by itself. You need to do some work on yourself too. Keep reading to learn my Keto weight loss tips.

MY WEIGHT LOSS TIPS WITH KETO

So, the Keto diet was what helped me to lose weight after a crazy number of times trying. Nothing else ever seemed to work. It didn't matter how determined I felt, or how religiously I stuck to the diet. Nothing worked.

Until Keto!
But, it would be a lie to say that it was Keto alone that helped me to shift the weight.

Because of course, I had a big part to play! It was hard, I needed to be smart, and I knew there'd be a long road ahead of me.

Here's how it happened.

I faced my issues
My weight problem wasn't just because I overate, ate the wrong foods, or didn't get enough exercise. It was about what was going on in my head. I started to ask myself why I made the food choices I did, how my weight was benefiting me (really, it was), and how to move through those issues.

So, whatever is the motivation behind the weight gain, even if it's for beauty purposes, you will have to address that issue at mind and make a change because you can still look jaw-dropping gorgeous with weight loss.

I didn't quit
Even with the most amazing diet in the world, you will experience hard times. I bet you, hard times are signs that you are making progress.

You might struggle with food cravings, battle those early detox symptoms and feel desperate when you think of avoiding sugar long-term. I certainly fought along the way.

But I never gave up. I pushed through the difficulties, I held my head high and pushed on through for myself and for everyone that admires me...wink! Looking at myself right now, it paid off!

I retrained my eating habits

I always had a huge appetite. Even in my thinner days, I'd polish off at least twice the amount that everyone else did. When I felt hungry, I ate.

All the diets I'd ever tried before were hard because I was continually feeling either deprived or hungry. But with Keto, I felt satisfied for longer.

I planned my meals

The worst time to decide what to eat is right before your meals when you're feeling hungry. Do this, and you're very likely to make poor food choices and opt for those high-carb, high-sugar, instant 'hit' foods.

That's why, when I got started, I carefully planned my meals throughout the day, compiled my grocery list and made sure I had everything that I needed to be healthy at home and stuck to my Keto lifestyle.

I kept a food diary

It's far too easy to forget what you've eaten and end up overeating in the course of a day. Forgetting to keep track of your macros (your fat, protein, and carbs) and making poor food choices may become inherent in your habits. So, track your food intake and macros by writing them down to give you control over what goes through your lips.

After a while, you'll be disciplined with the routine and will not need to write your intakes down.

I stayed flexible

OK, so this might sound strange for me to say, considering that I'm writing this book. Nevertheless, the truth is, Keto isn't a strict prescription that you need to stick to 100%. We're all different and have varying lifestyles and needs. A specific maximum number of carbs might be best for one person but be crazily high for you. Listen to your own body and give it what it needs.

I failed. But I kept going

I'm only human. I failed.

One day, I went on a date (my first in years, might I add!) and found myself munching on the free bread they provided while the conversation flowed. Eek! I stopped as soon as I realized my fall, but I still felt painfully guilty.

Then, the ultimate question came, should I quit eating now and save the progress, I'd made so far or do I ignore my previous Keto efforts and keep on with my bread? Guess, which option I chose?

I focused on me
About the same time when I went to Keto, one of my mother's friends took action to lose weight too. He chose the Keto diet and shifted weight quickly. It was amazing watching him shed those excess pounds and emerge leaner, healthier, more confident, and like a brand-new man.

How about me?
What was happening to my weight loss efforts – so slow? Was I doing something wrong? Should I give up before I make a fool of myself? NO! He had had a different body structure than mine hence the noticeable quick results.

A word of caution: in this age of Instagram, it's easy to forget that we aren't all supposed to be poster boys.

Being different is OK. Instead of thinking about other people and continually comparing my weight loss to theirs, I decided to be bold. I focused on myself instead.

Remember, weight loss isn't always linear. It can be, but more often than not, you might lose four pounds in one week and then gain another the next. Don't panic! It's all part of the journey.

The tips I've shared in this chapter should help you to keep pushing forward and making this shift to a brand new you.

Now that we've got all that out of the way let's talk about food. Sounds good? C'mon then!

Keto FAQs

How can I know that I am in ketosis?

There are some signs and symptoms like bad breath problems, increase your thirst and dry mouth, increase urination and rapid weight loss is the sign indicates that your body is in the state of ketosis.

How should I track my ketone level?

There are two methods to track ketones first one is urine test strips called keto strips. This is an inexpensive method to track ketone levels. Another method is blood test is one of the most accurate methods to track your ketone levels. This method is expensive you need keto meter and strips to track your blood ketone level.

How ketosis work in my body?

When we consume low carb foods our body uses fat as a primary energy source. Ketosis is the state in which your liver breakdown into molecules is known as ketones. These ketones are used by our bodies for energy. In this state your body breakdown fats for energy.

Is a keto diet being safe for diabetic people?

Yes, the keto diet helps to control blood sugar levels. Keto diet is a low carb diet it doesn't raise your blood sugar level.

Can I eat fruits during keto diet?

Most of the fruits are high in carb so you have to consume fruits which are low in carbs like you can eat avocados, coconut, olives, blackberries, raspberries, lemons, and tomatoes.

How long it takes to get me into ketosis?

When you start keto diet normally it takes 2 to 7 days' time to enter the state of ketosis. This time period is depending upon your eating habits, your body types, and your daily activity levels. Empty stomach exercise is one of the effective and fast ways to get enter into the state of ketosis.

SMOOTHIES & BREAKFAST

Breakfast Blueberry Coconut Smoothie

Serves: 2 |Ready in about: 5 minutes

Nutritional info per serving:

Calories: 492
Fat: 36.3g
Net Carbs: 8.6g
Protein: 9.6g

Ingredients:

- 1 avocado, pitted and sliced
- 2 cups blueberries
- 1 cup of coconut milk
- 6 tablespoons coconut cream
- 2 teaspoons erythritol
- 2 tablespoons coconut flakes

Instructions:

1. Combine the avocado slices, blueberries, coconut milk, coconut cream, erythritol, and ice cubes in a smoothie maker and blend until smooth.
2. Pour the smoothie into drinking glasses, and serve sprinkled with coconut flakes.

BLUEBERRY SMOOTHIE:

Serves: 1 | Ready in about: 5 minutes
Nutritional info per serving:

Calories: 215
Fat: 10g
Net Carbs: 7g
Protein: 23g

Ingredients:

- 1 cup Coconut Milk or almond milk
- ¼ cup Blueberries
- 1 teaspoon Vanilla Extract
- 1 teaspoon MCT Oil or coconut oil
- 30 grams Protein Powder (optional)

Instructions:

1. Blend all ingredients until smooth.

Morning Berry-Green Smoothie:

Serves: 4 | Ready in about: 5 minutes
Nutritional info per serving:

Calories: 360
Fat; 33.3g
Net Carbs: 6g
Protein: 6g

Ingredients:

- 1 avocado, pitted and sliced
- 3 cups mixed blueberries and strawberries
- 2 cups unsweetened almond milk
- 6 tablespoons heavy cream
- 2 teaspoons erythritol
- 1 cup of ice cubes
- ⅓ Cup nuts and seeds mix

Instructions:

2. Combine the avocado slices, blueberries, strawberries, almond milk, heavy cream, erythritol, ice cubes, nuts, and seeds in a smoothie maker; blend in high-speed until smooth and uniform.
3. Pour the smoothie into drinking glasses, and serve immediately.

Strawberry Smoothie:

Serves: 2 | Ready in about: 10 minutes
Nutritional info per serving:

Calories: 116
Fat: 9.6g
Net Carbs: 5g
Protein: 1g

Ingredients:

- 4 ounces of frozen strawberries
- 2 teaspoons Erythritol*
- ½ teaspoon organic vanilla extract
- 1/3 cup heavy whipping cream
- 1¼ cups unsweetened almond milk
- ½ cup of ice cubes

Instructions:

1. Place all the ingredients in a high-speed blender and pulse until smooth.
2. Pour the smoothie into serving glasses and serve.

Super food Red Smoothie:

Serves: 2 | Ready in about: 6 minutes
Nutritional info per serving:

Calories: 233
Fat: 4.3g
Net Carbs: 11.3g
Protein: 5g

Ingredients:

- 1 Granny Smith apple, peeled and chopped
- 1 cup strawberries + extra for garnishing
- 1 cup blueberries
- 2 small beets, peeled and chopped
- 2/3 cup ice cubes
- ½ lemon, juiced
- 2 cups almond milk

Instructions:

1. For the strawberries for garnishing, make a single deep cut on their sides, and set aside. In a smoothie maker, add the apples, strawberries, blueberries, beets, almond milk, and ice and blend the ingredients at high speed until nice and smooth, for about 75 seconds.
2. Add the lemon juice, and puree further for 30 seconds. Pour the drink into tall smoothie glasses, fix the reserved strawberries on each glass rim, and serve with a straw.

GREEN KETO SMOOTHIE:

Serves: 5 | Ready in about: 5 minutes
Nutritional info per serving:

Calories: 375
Fat: 25g
Net Carbs: 4g
Protein: 30g

Ingredients:

- 1 oz spinach
- 50 g cucumber
- 1 ½ cups almond milk
- 50 g celery
- 50 g avocado
- 1 tablespoon of coconut oil
- 10 drops of stevia liquid
- 1 scoop Isopure Protein Powder (approx. 30 g)
- ½ teaspoons Chia seeds (to garnish).
- 1 teaspoon matcha powder

Instructions:

1. Place almond milk and spinach in a blender or nutribullet. Mix spinach for a few seconds to make room for the rest of the ingredients.
2. Add the remaining ingredients and mix for a minute until creamy.
3. Garnish with chia seeds in a dish.

Bacon and Cheese Frittata:

Serves: 4 | Ready in about: 25 minutes
Nutritional info per serving:

Calories: 325
Fat: 28g
Net Carbs: 2g
Protein: 15g

Ingredients:

- 10 slices bacon
- 10 fresh eggs
- 3 tablespoons butter, melted
- ½ cup almond milk
- Salt and black pepper to taste
- 1 ½ cups cheddar cheese, shredded
- ¼ cup chopped green onions

Instructions:

1. Preheat the oven to 400°F and grease a baking dish with cooking spray.
2. Cook the bacon in a skillet over medium heat for 6 minutes.
3. Once crispy, remove from the skillet to paper towels and discard grease.
4. Chop into small pieces. Whisk the eggs, butter, milk, salt, and black pepper. Mix in the bacon and pour the mixture into the baking dish.
5. Sprinkle with cheddar cheese and green onions, and bake in the oven for 10 minutes or until the eggs are thoroughly cooked.
6. Remove and cool the frittata for 3 minutes, slice into wedges, and serve warm with a dollop of Greek yogurt.

Blueberry Bread:

Serves: 8 |Ready in about: 1 hour
Nutritional info per serving:

Calories: 196
Fat: 12.8g
Net Carbs: 2.7g
Protein: 5.4g

Ingredients:

- ½ cup almond flour
- 2 teaspoons organic baking powder
- ½ teaspoon salt
- 5 organic eggs
- ½ cup unsweetened almond milk
- ½ cup almond butter, melted
- ½ cup unsalted butter, melted
- ½ cup fresh blueberries

Instructions:

1. Preheat the oven to 350°F. Line a loaf pan with parchment paper.
2. In a bowl, mix well flour, baking powder, and salt.
3. Add the eggs and almond milk in a second bowl and beat well.
4. In a third bowl, mix together the almond butter and butter.
5. Now, add the flour mixture and mix until well combined.
6. Add the egg mixture and mix until well combined.
7. Gently, fold in the blueberries.
8. Place mixture evenly into the prepared bread loaf pan and with your hands, press to smooth the top surface.
9. Bake for 45 minutes or until a wooden skewer inserted in the center comes out clean.
10. Remove the loaf pan from the oven and place onto a wire rack to cool for about 10 minutes.
11. Carefully, invert the bread onto a wire rack to cool completely before slicing.
12. With a sharp knife, cut the bread loaf into 8 equal-sized slices and serve.

Creamy Vanilla Keto Cappuccino:

Serves: 2 | Ready in about: 6 minutes
Nutritional info per serving:

Calories: 253
Fat: 17.7g
Net Carbs: 6.2g
Protein: 12.8g

Ingredients:

- 2 cups unsweetened vanilla almond milk, chilled
- 1 teaspoon swerve sugar
- ½ tablespoon powdered coffee
- 1 cup cottage cheese, cold
- ½ teaspoon vanilla bean paste
- ¼ teaspoon xanthan gum
- Unsweetened chocolate shavings to garnish

Instructions:

1. In a blender, combine the almond milk, swerve sugar, cottage cheese, coffee, vanilla bean paste, and xanthan gum and process on high speed for 1 minute until smooth.
2. Pour into tall shake glasses, sprinkle with chocolate shavings, and serve immediately.

KETO CHEESE OMELET:

Serves: 2 | Ready in about: 15 minutes
Nutritional info per serving:

Calories: 897
Fat: 80g
Net Carbs: 4g
Protein: 40g

Ingredients:

- 3 oz butter
- 6 eggs
- Salt and pepper to taste
- 7 oz shredded cheddar cheese

Instructions:

1. Mix the eggs smoothly, and then blend in half of the cheddar.
2. Melt the butter in a hot frying pan, pour the egg mixture and leave for a few mins
3. Reduce the heat and add the remaining shredded cheese.
4. Fold the omelet and serve immediately.

Ham & Egg Broccoli Bake:

Serves: 4 | Ready in about: 25 minutes
Nutritional info per serving:

Calories: 344
Fat: 28g
Net Carbs: 4.2g
Protein: 11g

Ingredients:

- 2 heads broccoli, cut into small florets
- 2 red bell peppers, seeded and chopped
- ¼ cup chopped ham
- 2 teaspoons ghee
- 1 teaspoon dried oregano + extra to garnish
- Salt and black pepper to taste
- 8 fresh eggs

Instructions:

1. Preheat oven to 425°F.
2. Melt the ghee in a frying pan over medium heat; brown the ham, stirring frequently, about 3 minutes.
3. Arrange the broccoli, bell peppers, and ham on a foil-lined baking sheet in a single layer, toss to combine; season with salt, oregano, and black pepper. Bake for 10 minutes until the vegetables have softened.
4. Remove, create eight indentations with a spoon, and crack an egg into each. Return to the oven and continue to bake for an additional 5 to 7 minutes until the egg whites are firm.
5. Season with salt, black pepper, and extra oregano, share the bake into four plates and serve with strawberry lemonade (optional).

Bacon Omelet:

Serves: 1 | Ready in about: 29 minutes

Nutritional info per serving:

Calories: 466
Net Carbs: 1.6g
Fat: 37.2g
Protein: 30.5g

Ingredients:

- 1 bacon slice
- ½ tablespoon butter
- 2 large organic eggs
- ½ tablespoon fresh chives, minced
- Ground black pepper, as required
- 1-ounce cheddar cheese, shredded

Instructions:

1. Heat a nonstick small skillet over medium-high heat and cook the bacon slice for about 8-10 minutes, stirring frequently.
2. With a slotted spoon, transfer the bacon onto a paper towel-lined plate to drain.
3. Then, chop the bacon slice.
4. Remove the bacon grease from the frying pan and then, wipe it using a paper towel.
5. In a bowl, add the eggs, chives, and black pepper and beat until well combined.
6. In the same frypan, melt the butter over medium-low heat.
7. Add the egg mixture and cook for about 2 minutes.
8. Carefully, flip the side of omelet and top with chopped bacon.
9. Cook for about 1-2 minutes or until the desired doneness of eggs.
10. Remove from heat and immediately, add cheese in the center of the omelet.
11. Fold the edges of omelet over cheese.
12. Serve immediately.

Yummy Blue Cheese & Mushroom Omelet:

Serves: 2 | Ready in about: 15 minutes
Nutritional info per serving:

Calories: 310
Fat: 25g
Net Carbs: 1.5g
Protein: 18.5g

Ingredients:

- 4 eggs, beaten
- 4 button mushrooms, sliced
- Salt, to taste
- 1 tablespoon olive oil
- ½ cup blue cheese, crumbled
- 1 tomato, thinly sliced
- 1 tablespoon parsley, chopped

Instructions:

1. Set a pan over medium heat and warm the oil.
2. Sauté the mushrooms for 5 minutes until tender; season with salt. Add in the eggs and cook as you swirl them around the pan using a spatula.
3. Cook eggs until partially set. Top with cheese; fold the omelet in half to enclose filling. Decorate with tomato and parsley and serve warm.

POULTRY

Rosemary Chicken with Avocado Sauce:

Serves: 2 | Ready in about: 22 minutes
Nutritional info per serving:

Calories: 406
Fat: 34.1g
Net Carbs: 3.9g
Protein: 22.3g

Ingredients:

Sauce:
- ¼ cup mayonnaise
- 1 avocado, pitted
- 1 tablespoon lemon juice
- Salt to taste

Chicken:
- 2 tablespoons olive oil
- 2 chicken breasts
- Salt and black pepper to taste
- ½ cup rosemary, chopped
- ¼ cup of warm water

Instructions:

1. Mash the avocado with a fork, in a bowl, and add in mayonnaise and lemon juice.
2. Warm olive oil in a large skillet, season the chicken with salt and black pepper and fry for 4 minutes on each side to a golden brown. Remove the chicken to a plate.
3. Pour the warm water in the same skillet and add the rosemary. Bring to simmer for 3 minutes and add the chicken. Cover and cook on low heat for 5 minutes until the liquid has reduced and chicken is fragrant.
4. Dish chicken into serving plates and spoon the avocado sauce over.

FRIED MARINATED CHICKEN:

Serves: 4 | Ready in about: 3 hours 5 minutes
Nutritional info per serving:

Calories: 117
Fat: 5g
Net Carbs: 0g
Protein: 16g

Ingredients:

- Cooking oil
- 1-kilo chicken; cut into desired pieces
- 6 tablespoons fish sauce (patis)
- ¼ tablespoon ground black pepper
- 1 lemon

Instructions:

1. Mix fish sauce, pepper, and lemon juice and marinate chicken for 3 hours.
2. Deep fry until golden brown in hot cooking oil.

Spinach Chicken Cheesy Bake:

Serves: 6 |Ready in about: 45 minutes
Nutritional info per serving:

Calories: 340
Fat: 30.2g
Net Carbs: 3.1g
Protein: 15g

Ingredients:

- 6 chicken breasts, skinless and boneless
- 1 teaspoon mixed spice seasoning
- Pink salt and black pepper to season
- 2 loose cups baby spinach
- 3 teaspoons olive oil
- 4 oz cream cheese, cubed
- 1 ¼ cups shredded mozzarella cheese
- 4 tablespoons water

Instructions:

1. Preheat oven to 370°F.
2. Season chicken with spice mix, salt, and black pepper. Pat with your hands to have the seasoning stick on the chicken.
3. Put in the casserole dish and layer spinach over the chicken.
4. Mix the oil with cream cheese, mozzarella, salt, and black pepper and stir in water a tablespoon at a time.
5. Pour the mixture over the chicken and cover the pot with aluminum foil.
6. Bake for 20 minutes, remove foil and continue cooking for 15 minutes until a nice golden brown color is formed on top. Take out and allow sitting for 5 minutes. Serve warm with braised asparagus.

Roasted Whole Chicken:

Serves: 4 | Ready in about: 1 hour 52 minutes

Nutritional info per serving:

Calories: 772
Fat: 39.1g
Net Carbs: 0.7g
Protein: 99g

Ingredients:

- 10 tablespoons unsalted butter
- 3 garlic cloves, minced
- 1 (3-pounds) grass-fed whole chicken, neck, and giblets removed
- Salt and ground black pepper, as required

Instructions:

1. Preheat the oven to 400°F. Arrange an oven rack into the lower portion of the oven.
2. Grease a large baking dish.
3. Place the butter and garlic in a small pan over medium heat and cook for about 1-2 minutes.
4. Remove the pan from heat and let it cool for about 2 minutes.
5. Season the inside and outside of chicken evenly with salt and black pepper.
6. Arrange the chicken into a prepared baking dish, breast side up.
7. Pour the garlic butter over and inside of the chicken.
8. Bake for about 1-1½ hours, basting with the pan juices every 20 minutes.
9. Remove from oven and place the chicken onto a cutting board for about 5-10 minutes before carving.
10. Cut into desired size pieces and serve.

Green Bean & Broccoli Chicken Stir-Fry:

Serves: 2 |Ready in about: 30 minutes
Nutritional info per serving:

Calories: 411
Fat: 24.5g
Net Carbs: 6.2g
Protein: 28.3g

Ingredients:

- 2 chicken breasts, skinless, boneless, cut into strips
- 2 tablespoons olive oil
- 1 teaspoon red pepper flakes
- 1 teaspoon onion powder
- 1 tablespoon fresh ginger, grated
- ¼ cup tamari sauce
- ½ teaspoon garlic powder
- ½ cup of water
- ½ cup xylitol
- 2 oz green beans, chopped
- ½ teaspoon xanthan gum
- ½ cup green onions, chopped
- ½ head broccoli, cut into florets

Instructions:

1. In a pot, steam green beans in salted water for 2-3 minutes; set aside.
2. Set a pan over medium heat and warm oil, cook in the chicken, and ginger for 4 minutes. Stir in the water, onion powder, pepper flakes, garlic powder, tamari sauce, xanthan gum, and xylitol, and cook for 15 minutes.
3. Add in the green onions, green beans, and broccoli, and cook for 6 minutes.

BUFFALO CHICKEN PIZZA:

Serves: 5 | Ready in about: 10 minutes
Nutritional info per serving:

Calories: 365
Fat: 11g
Net Carbs: 42g
Protein: 24g

Ingredients:

- Vegetable cooking spray
- ½ cup Buffalo-style hot sauce
- 1 (16-oz) package prebaked Italian pizza crust
- 2 cups chopped deli-roasted whole chicken
- 1 cup (4 oz) shredded Provolone cheese
- ¼ cup crumbled blue cheese

Instructions:

1. Coat the grill with the spray and put it on the grill. Preheat grill to 350° F (medium heat).
2. Spread the hot sauce over the crust, and the next 3 ingredients surface.
3. Place the crust on the cooking grate directly. Grill at 350° F (medium heat) for 4 min, covered with the grill lid.
4. Rotate 1-quarter turn pizza and grill, covered with grill top, for 5 to 6 min or until heated thoroughly. Serve right away.

Spinach & Ricotta Stuffed Chicken Breasts:

Serves: 3 |Ready in about: 25 minutes
Nutritional info per serving:

Calories: 305
Fat: 12g
Net Carbs: 4g
Protein: 23g

Ingredients:

- 1 cup spinach, cooked and chopped
- 3 chicken breasts
- Salt and ground black pepper, to taste
- 4 ounces cream cheese, softened
- 1/2 cup ricotta cheese, crumbled
- 1 garlic clove, peeled and minced
- 1 tablespoon coconut oil
- ½ cup white wine

Instructions:

1. In a bowl, combine the ricotta cheese with cream cheese, salt, garlic, pepper, and spinach.
2. Add the chicken breasts on a working surface, cut a pocket in each, stuff them with the spinach mixture, and add more pepper and salt.
3. Set a pan over medium heat and warm oil, add the stuffed chicken, and cook each side for 5 minutes.
4. Put in a baking tray, drizzle with white wine and 2 tablespoons of water, and then place in the oven at 420°F.
5. Bake for 10 minutes, arrange on a serving plate, and serve.

Tangy Chicken Breasts:

Serves: 4 | Ready in about: 29 minutes
Nutritional info per serving:

Calories: 378
Fat: 18.4g
Net Carbs: 0.3g
Protein: 49.3g

Ingredients:

- ¼ cup balsamic vinegar
- 2 tablespoons butter, melted
- 1½ teaspoons fresh lemon juice
- ½ teaspoon lemon-pepper seasoning
- 4 (6-ounces) grass-fed boneless, skinless chicken breast halves, pounded slightly

Instructions:

1. Place the vinegar, butter, lemon juice, and seasoning into a glass baking dish and mix well.
2. Add the chicken breasts and generously, coat with the mixture.
3. Refrigerate to marinate for about 25-30 minutes.
4. Preheat the grill to medium heat. Grease the grill grate.
5. Remove the chicken from the bowl and discard the remaining marinade.
6. Place the chicken breasts onto the grill and cover with the lid.
7. Cook for about 5-7 minutes per side or until desired doneness.
8. Serve hot.

Hot Chicken Meatballs:

Serves: 2 | Ready in about: 25 minutes

Nutritional info per serving:

Calories: 487
Fat: 35g
Net Carbs: 4.3g,
Protein: 31.5g

Ingredients:

- 1 pound ground chicken
- Salt and black pepper, to taste
- 2 tablespoons yellow mustard
- ½ cup almond flour
- ¼ cup mozzarella cheese, grated
- ¼ cup hot sauce
- 1 egg

Instructions:

1. Preheat oven to 400°F and line a baking tray with parchment paper.
2. In a bowl, combine the chicken, black pepper, mustard, flour, mozzarella cheese, salt, and egg. Form meatballs and arrange them on the baking tray.
3. Cook for 16 minutes, then pour over the hot sauce and bake for 5 more minutes.

KETO CHICKEN ENCHILADAS:

Serves: 6 | Ready in about: 20 minutes
Nutritional info per serving:

Calories: 349
Fat: 19g
Net Carbs: 9g
Protein: 31g

Ingredients:

- 2 cups gluten-free enchilada sauce
- Chicken
- 1 tablespoon Avocado oil
- 4 cloves Garlic (minced)
- 3 cups Shredded chicken (cooked)
- ¼ cup Chicken broth
- ¼ cup fresh cilantro (chopped)

Assembly
- 12 Coconut tortillas
- 3/4 cup Colby jack cheese (shredded)
- ¼ cup Green onions (chopped)

Instructions:

1. Heat oil over medium to high heat in a large pan. Add the chopped garlic and cook until fragrant for about a minute.
2. Add rice, 1 cup enchilada sauce (half the total), chicken, and coriander. Simmer for 5 minutes.
3. In the meantime, heat the oven to 375⁰ F. Grease a 9x13 baking dish.
4. In the middle of each tortilla, place ¼ cup chicken mixture. Roll up and place seam side down in the baking dish.
5. Pour the remaining cup enchilada sauce over the enchiladas. Sprinkle with shredded cheese.
6. Bake for 10 to 12 minutes Sprinkle with green onions.

Spicy Chicken Leg Quarters:

Serves: 3 | Ready in about: 1 hour 8 minutes

Nutritional info per serving:

Calories: 725
Fat: 59.7g
Net Carbs: 0.4g
Protein: 48.3g

Ingredients:

- 3 (10-11 ounces) grass-fed bone-in, skin-on chicken leg quarters
- ½ cup mayonnaise
- 1 teaspoon paprika
- ½ teaspoon garlic powder
- Salt and ground white pepper, as required

Instructions:

1. Preheat the oven to 350°F. Generously, grease a baking dish.
2. Add the mayonnaise in a shallow bowl.
3. Place the paprika, garlic powder, salt, and white pepper in a small bowl and mix well.
4. Coat each chicken quarter with mayonnaise and then, sprinkle evenly with the spice mixture.
5. Arrange the chicken quarters onto the prepared baking sheet in a single layer.
6. Bake for about 45 minutes.
7. Now, increase the temperature of the oven to 4000 F and bake for about 5-8 more minutes.
8. Remove from the oven and place the chicken quarters onto a platter.
9. With a piece of foil, cover each chicken quarter loosely for about 5-10 minutes before serving.
10. Serve.

Stuffed Avocados with Chicken:

Serves: 2 | Ready in about: 10 minutes
Nutritional info per serving:

Calories: 511
Fat: 40g
Net Carbs: 5g
Protein: 24g

Ingredients:

- 2 avocados, cut in half and pitted
- ¼ cup pesto
- 2 tablespoons cream cheese
- 1½ cups chicken, cooked and shredded
- ¼ teaspoon cayenne pepper
- ½ teaspoon onion powder
- ½ teaspoon garlic powder
- 1 teaspoon paprika
- Salt and black pepper, to taste
- 2 tablespoons lemon juice

Instructions:

1. Scoop the insides of the avocado halves, and place the flesh in a bowl.
2. Add in the chicken and stir in the remaining ingredients.
3. Stuff the avocado cups with chicken mixture and enjoy.

KETO GLUTEN-FREE CHICKEN AND DUMPLINGS:

Serves: 8 | Ready in about: 20 minutes

Nutritional info per serving:

Calories: 273
Fat: 14g
Net Carbs: 5g
Protein: 28g

Ingredients:

- 1 tablespoon Olive oil
- ½ large Onion
- 1 large Carrot
- 1 stalk Celery
- 2 teaspoons Italian seasoning
- 1 ½ lb Chicken breast
- 8 cups Chicken broth
- 2 medium Dried bay leaves
- ½ Fathead bagel dough

Instructions:

1. Heat olive oil, and sauté potatoes, onions and celery for about 10 minutes.
2. Add Italian seasoning, chicken, chicken broth, and Bay leaves. Cook 6 minutes in a pressure cooker.
3. While, use the same instructions and quantities as the fathead bagels to make fathead bread, except to break the method in half. (Either enters "3" in the bagel serving box, OR make the whole dough, but use only half of it for keto chicken and dumplings.)
4. If the dough is soft, refrigerate until firm for approximately 20 minutes.
5. Place the fathead dough between 2 parchment paper pieces. Roll out, about ¼ in (.5 cm) thick, to a rectangle. Cut into strips with a width of about 2 in (5 cm)x ½ in (1 cm).
6. Remove the lid when the soup is done, and pressure is released. Remove leaves from the harbor.
7. Cut the chicken and cut it into bite-sized pieces.
8. Set the Sauté mode to the Instant Pot again. Disable for approximately 3 minutes before cooking.

BEEF & LAMB

Asian Spiced Beef with Broccoli:

Serves: 2 | Ready in about: 30 minutes
Nutritional info per serving:

Calories: 623
Fat: 43.2g
Net Carbs: 2.3g
Protein: 53.5g

Ingredients:

- ½ cup of coconut milk
- 2 tablespoons coconut oil
- ¼ teaspoon garlic powder
- ¼ teaspoon onion powder
- ½ tablespoon coconut aminos
- 1 pound beef steak, cut into strips
- Salt and black pepper, to taste
- 1 head broccoli, cut into florets
- ½ tablespoon Thai green curry paste
- 1 teaspoon ginger paste
- 1 tablespoon cilantro, chopped
- ½ tablespoon sesame seeds

Instructions:

1. Warm coconut oil in a pan over medium heat, add in the beef, season with garlic powder, black pepper, salt, ginger paste, and onion powder and cook for 4 minutes.
2. Mix in the broccoli and stir-fry for 5 minutes.
3. Pour in the coconut milk, coconut aminos, and Thai curry paste and cook for 15 minutes.
4. Serve sprinkled with cilantro and sesame seeds.

KETO BEEF LASAGNA:

Serves: 6 | Ready in about: 1 hour
Nutritional info per serving:

Calories: 514.1
Fat: 28.5g
Net Carbs: 4.9g
Protein: 21.1g

Ingredients:

- 1 lb ground beef
- ½ lb Italian sausage
- ¼ cup chopped white onion
- 1 ½ cups marinara sauce
- 3/4 teaspoons garlic powder, divided
- 1 teaspoon oregano, divided
- ½ cup ricotta cheese
- 1 cup grated mozzarella, divided
- 2/3 cup parmesan, divided
- Chopped parsley for garnish (optional)

Instructions:

1. Preheat the oven to 400°F.
2. In a 12-inch cast-iron skillet (or similar oven-proof equivalent), brown the ground meat and the ground sausage over medium heat on the stove until it isn't pink (about 15 minutes). Drain off excess fat and heat again.
3. Put the onions in the pan and fry it with meat until it starts to soften for 3 to 5 minutes For the sauce, ½ teaspoon oregano and ½ teaspoon garlic powder into the pan with the meat sauce and simmer for 5 minutes.
4. Combine ricotta, ½ cup mozzarella, and ⅓ cup parmesan in a medium bowl. Add a slight salt and pepper to taste and add the remaining oregano and garlic powder to the cheese mixture and fold until everything is well combined.
5. Turn off the heat and spread the meat over the pan until a uniform layer is left. Place the tablespoon the cheese mixture around the pan; push them a little with your spoon at the bottom of the pan.
6. Sprinkle the top with the rest of the mozzarella and parmesan. Bake for 20 minutes until boiling, and the top begins to brown. Garnish with chopped parsley, if desired. Serve hot.

Italian Beef Ragout:

Serves: 4 | Ready in about: 1 hour 52 minutes
Nutritional info per serving:

Calories: 328
Fat: 21.6g
Net Carbs: 4.2g
Protein: 36.6g

Ingredients:

- 1 lb chuck steak, trimmed and cubed
- 2 tablespoons olive oil
- Salt and black pepper to taste
- 2 tablespoons almond flour
- 1 medium onion, diced
- ½ cup dry white wine
- 1 red bell pepper, seeded and diced
- 2 teaspoons Worcestershire sauce
- 4 oz tomato puree
- 3 teaspoons smoked paprika
- 1 cup beef broth
- Thyme leaves to garnish

Instructions:

1. First, lightly dredge the meat in the almond flour and set aside.
2. Place a large skillet over medium heat, add 1 tablespoon of oil to heat and then sauté the onion, and bell pepper for 3 minutes.
3. Stir in the paprika, and add the remaining olive oil.
4. Add the beef and cook for 10 minutes in total while turning them halfway.
5. Stir in white wine, let it reduce by half, about 3 minutes, and add Worcestershire sauce, tomato puree, and beef broth.
6. Let the mixture boil for 2 minutes, then reduce the heat to lowest and let simmer for 1 ½ hour; stirring now and then.
7. Adjust the taste and dish the ragout. Serve garnished with thyme leaves.

Cocktail Chili Beef Meatballs:

Serves: 2-4 | Ready in about: 45 minutes
Nutritional info per serving:

Calories: 341
Fat: 21g
Net Carbs: 5.6g
Protein: 23.5g

Ingredients:

- 2 tablespoons olive oil
- 2 tablespoons thyme
- ½ cup pork rinds, crushed
- 1 egg
- Salt and black pepper, to taste
- 1½ pounds ground beef
- 10 ounces canned onion soup
- 1 tablespoon almond flour
- 2 tablespoons chili sauce
- ¼ cup free-sugar ketchup
- 3 teaspoons Worcestershire sauce
- ½ teaspoon dry mustard

Instructions:

1. In a bowl, combine 1/3 cup of the onion soup with beef, pepper, thyme, pork rinds, egg, and salt.
2. Shape meatballs from the beef mixture. Heat olive oil in a pan over medium heat and place in the meatballs to brown on both sides.
3. In a bowl, combine the rest of the soup with the almond flour, dry mustard, ketchup, Worcestershire sauce, and ¼ cup of water.
4. Pour this over the beef meatballs, cover the pan, and cook for 20 minutes.

KETO INSTANT POT BEEF STEW:

Serves: 6 | Ready in about: 1 hour 5 minutes

Nutritional info per serving:

Calories: 437
Fat: 32g
Net Carbs: 6g
Protein: 28g

Ingredients:

- 4 tablespoons olive oil, separated
- Cut 3 lbs of beef into 2-inch cubes
- ½ teaspoon salt
- ¼ teaspoon ground black pepper
- 1 medium-sized yellow onion, chopped
- 2 large carrots, chopped
- 2 chopped celery stalks
- 10 large radishes cut in half
- 5g of crimini mushrooms, quartered
- garlic cloves
- ½ teaspoon dried thyme
- 3 tablespoons tomato puree
- 2 cups of beef broth
- chopped fresh parsley (optional to garnish)

Instruction:

1. Place all ingredients in a pressure cooker.
2. Securely close the lid and press the Stew option. It should cook for about an hour.
3. After depressurizing, carefully open the lid.
4. Top with chopped parsley.

Beef with Dilled Yogurt:

Serves: 6 | Ready in about: 25 minutes
Nutritional info per serving:

Calories: 408
Fat: 22.4g
Net Carbs: 8.3g
Protein: 27g

Ingredients:

- ¼ cup almond milk
- 2 pounds ground beef
- 1 onion, grated
- 5 zero carb bread slices, torn
- 1 egg, whisked
- ¼ cup fresh parsley, chopped
- Salt and black pepper, to taste
- 2 garlic cloves, minced
- ¼ cup fresh mint, chopped
- 2 ½ teaspoons dried oregano
- ¼ cup olive oil
- 1 cup cherry tomatoes, halved
- 1 cucumber, sliced
- 1 cup baby spinach
- 1½ tablespoons lemon juice
- 1 cup dilled Greek yogurt

Instruction:

1. Place the torn bread in a bowl, add in the milk, and set aside for 3 minutes.
2. Squeeze the bread, chop, and place into a bowl. Stir in the beef, salt, mint, onion, parsley, pepper, egg, oregano, and garlic.
3. Form balls out of this mixture and place them on a working surface.
4. Set a pan over medium heat and warm half of the oil; fry the meatballs for 8 minutes. Flip occasionally, and set aside in a tray.
5. On a salad plate, combine the spinach with the cherry tomatoes and cucumber.
6. Mix in the remaining oil, lemon juice, black pepper, and salt. Spread dilled yogurt over, and top with meatballs to serve.

Lamb Curry:

Serves: 4 | Ready in about: 2 hours 5 minutes

Nutritional info per serving:

Calories: 410
Fat: 27.3g
Net Carbs: 5.8g
Protein: 34g

Ingredients:

- 1 tablespoon olive oil
- 1 pound grass-fed boneless lamb, cubed
- 1 celery stalk, chopped
- 1 small yellow onion, chopped
- 1/3 of fresh red chili, chopped
- 1 teaspoon butter
- 2 garlic cloves, minced
- 2 teaspoons graham masala powder
- 1 teaspoon red chili powder
- ¼ teaspoon ground turmeric
- 1 tablespoon sugar-free tomato paste
- 1 cup unsweetened coconut milk
- ½ cup of water
- 1 medium carrot, peeled and chopped
- 1 teaspoon fresh lime juice
- Salt and ground black pepper, as required
- 2 tablespoons fresh cilantro leaves, chopped

Instructions:

1. In a large pan, heat the oil over high heat and sear the lamb cubes for about 4-5 minutes.
2. Add the onion, celery, and red chili and cook for about 1 minute.
3. Now, adjust the heat to medium.
4. Stir in the butter, garlic, and spices and cook for about 1 minute.
5. Stir in the tomato paste, coconut milk, and water and bring to a boil.
6. Adjust the heat to low and simmer, covered for about 1 hour, stirring occasionally.
7. Stir in the carrot and simmer, covered for about 40 minutes.
8. Stir in the lime juice, salt, and black pepper and remove from heat.
9. Garnish with fresh cilantro and serve hot.

Lamb Kebabs with Mint Yogurt:

Serves: 2 | Ready in about: 20 minutes
Nutritional info per serving:

Calories: 543
Fat: 33.5g
Net Carbs: 4.7g
Protein: 52.5g

Ingredients:

- 1 pound ground lamb
- ¼ teaspoon cinnamon
- 1 teaspoon garlic powder
- 1 teaspoon onion powder
- Salt and black pepper, to taste
- 1 cup natural yogurt
- 2 tablespoons mint, chopped

Instructions:

1. Preheat your grill to medium heat.
2. Place lamb, cinnamon, onion powder, salt, and black pepper in a bowl. Mix with hands to combine well.
3. Divide the meat into pieces. Shape all meat portions around previously-soaked skewers and grill the kebabs for about 5 minutes per side.
4. In a separate bowl, put the yogurt, garlic powder, mint, and salt and stir to combine.

GRILLED CHERMOULA LAMB CHOPS:

Serves: 4 | Ready in about: 20 minutes
Nutritional info per serving:

Calories: 392
Fat: 14g
Net Carbs: 1.5g
Protein: 31g

Ingredients:

- 8 lamb chops
- 1 teaspoon vegetable oil
- 2 tablespoons Resell Hangout
- Leaf

For the Chermoula:
- 2 tablespoons fresh mint, chopped
- ¼ cup fresh parsley, minced
- 2 tablespoons lemon peel
- 3 cloves of garlic, finely chopped
- ½ teaspoon smoked pepper (regularly consume if you've got not smoked)
- 1 teaspoon red pepper flakes
- ¼ cup of vegetable oil
- 2 tablespoons juice
- Salt and pepper to taste

Instructions:

1. Rub the lamb with vegetable oil and canopy the handout and salt. (If you are doing not use resell hangout, season generously with salt, pepper, and touch cumin).
2. Preheat your grill and cook about 2 minutes on all sides.
3. Let the meat sit for a couple of minutes before serving.
4. For the Chermoula:
5. Mix all Chermoula ingredients during a kitchen appliance and squeeze until you get a consistency that appears like pesto. Don't mix too much; it must not be completely liquid.
6. Serve lamb chops with a generous portion of Chermoula and slightly fresh lemon rind

North African Lamb:

Serves: 4 | Ready in about: 25 minutes
Nutritional info per serving:

Calories: 445
Fat: 32g
Net Carbs: 4g
Protein: 34g

Ingredients:

- 2 teaspoons paprika
- 2 garlic cloves, minced
- 2 teaspoons dried oregano
- 2 tablespoons sumac
- 12 lamb cutlets
- ¼ cup sesame oil
- 2 teaspoons cumin
- 4 carrots, sliced
- ¼ cup fresh parsley, chopped
- 2 teaspoons harissa paste
- 1 tablespoon red wine vinegar
- Salt and black pepper, to taste
- 2 tablespoons black olives, sliced
- 2 cucumbers, sliced

Instructions:

1. In a bowl, combine the cutlets with the paprika, oregano, black pepper, 2 tablespoons water, half of the oil, sumac, garlic, and salt, and rub well.
2. Add the carrots in a pot, cover with water, bring to a boil over medium heat, cook for 2 minutes then drain before placing them in a salad bowl.
3. Place the cucumbers and olives to the carrots.
4. In another bowl, combine the harissa with the rest of the oil, a splash of water, parsley, vinegar, and cumin. Place this to the carrots mixture, season with pepper and salt, and toss well to coat.
5. Preheat the grill to medium heat and arrange the lamb cutlets on it, grill each side for 3 minutes, and split among separate plates. Serve alongside the carrot salad.

Broiled Lamb Chops:

Serves: 4 | Ready in about: 23 minutes
Nutritional info per serving:

Calories: 477
Fat: 21.1g
Net Carbs: 2g
Protein: 65.2g

Ingredients:

- 2 tablespoons garlic, minced
- 2 tablespoons fresh oregano, minced
- ½ teaspoon fresh lemon zest, finely grated
- 1 tablespoon olive oil
- 2 tablespoons fresh lemon juice
- Salt and ground black pepper, as required
- 8 (4-ounces) grass-fed lamb loin chops, trimmed
- 2 tablespoons Parmesan cheese, shredded

Instructions:

1. Place all the ingredients except lamb chops and Parmesan in a large baking dish and mix until well combined.
2. Add the chops and generously coat with garlic mixture.
3. Cover the baking dish and refrigerate to marinate for at least 1 hour.
4. Preheat the broiler of oven to high heat. Grease a broiler pan.
5. Arrange the chops onto prepared broiler pan in a single layer.
6. Broil for about 3-4 minutes per side.
7. Sprinkle with Parmesan cheese and serve hot.

Stuffed Lamb Shoulder:

Serves: 2-4 | Ready in about: 1 hour
Nutritional info per serving:

Calories: 557
Fat: 41g
Net Carbs: 3.1g
Protein: 37g

Ingredients:

- 2 tablespoons olive oil
- 1 lb. rolled lamb shoulder, boneless
- 1 ½ cups basil leaves, chopped
- 5 tablespoons macadamia nuts, chopped
- ½ cup green olives, pitted and chopped
- 2 garlic cloves, minced
- Salt and black pepper to taste

Instructions:

1. In a bowl, combine the basil, macadamia nuts, olives, and garlic.
2. Season the lamb with salt and black pepper.
3. Spread with the previously prepared mixture, roll up the lamb and tie it together using 3 to 4 strings of butcher's twine.
4. Place the lamb onto a greased with olive oil baking dish and cook in the oven for 10 minutes at 420^0 F. Reduce the heat to 350^0 F and continue cooking for 40 minutes.
5. When ready, transfer the meat to a cleaned chopping board, and let it rest for 10 minutes before slicing.

LAMB SLIDERS:

Serves: 6 | Ready in about: 20 minutes

Nutritional info per serving:

Calories: 216
Fat: 17g
Net Carbs: 1.6g
Protein: 12 g

Ingredients:

- 1 lb. minced lamb or half veal, half lamb
- ½ sliced onion
- 2 garlic cloves minced
- 1 tablespoon dried dill
- 1 teaspoon salt
- ½ teaspoon black pepper

Instructions:

1. Mix the ingredients gently in a large bowl until well combined. Overworking the meat will cause it to be tough.
2. Shape the meat into burgers.
3. Grill or fry in a pan over medium-high heat until cooked through, 4-5 minutes per side. If preparing in a pan, I like to quickly sear both sides then throw the burgers in a 350° F oven for 10 min to finish cooking through.
4. Serve with Tzatziki for dipping!

PORK

Barbecued Pork Chops:

Serves: 2 | Ready in about: 20 minutes
Nutritional info per serving:

Calories: 412
Fat: 34.6 g
Net Carbs: 1.1 g
Protein: 34.1 g

Ingredients:

- 2 pork loin chops, boneless
- ½ cup BBQ sauce, sugar-free
- Salt and black pepper to taste
- 1 tablespoon erythritol
- ½ teaspoon ginger powder
- ½ teaspoon onion powder
- ½ teaspoon garlic powder
- 1 teaspoon red pepper flakes
- 2 thyme sprigs, chopped

Instructions:

1. Mix black pepper, salt, ginger powder, onion powder, garlic powder and red pepper flakes, and rub the pork chops on all sides. Preheat the grill to 450° F and cook the meat for 2 minutes per side.
2. Reduce the heat and brush the BBQ sauce on the meat, cover and grill for another 5 minutes.
3. Open the lid, turn the meat and brush again with barbecue sauce.
4. Continue cooking covered for 5 minutes. Remove the meat to a serving platter and serve sprinkled with thyme.

Pork Sausage Bake:

Serves: 4 | Ready in about: 50 minutes
Nutritional info per serving:

Calories: 465
Fat: 41.6g
Net Carbs: 4.4g
Protein: 15.1g

Ingredients:

- 12 pork sausages
- 5 large tomatoes cut in rings
- 1 red bell pepper, seeded and sliced
- 1 yellow bell pepper, seeded and sliced
- 1 green bell pepper, seeded and sliced
- 1 sprig thyme, chopped
- 1 sprig rosemary, chopped
- 4 cloves garlic, minced
- 2 bay leaves
- 1 tablespoon olive oil
- 2 tablespoons balsamic vinegar

Instructions:

1. Preheat the oven to 350°F.
2. In the cast iron pan, add the tomatoes, bell peppers, thyme, rosemary, garlic, bay leaves, olive oil, and balsamic vinegar. Toss everything and arrange the sausages on top of the veggies.
3. Put the pan within the oven and bake for 20 minutes. After, remove the pan shake it a bit and turn the sausages over with a spoon. Continue cooking for 25 minutes or until the sausages have browned to your desired color. Serve with the veggie and cooking sauce with cauli rice.

Pork Stroganoff:

Serves: 5 | Ready in about: 55 minutes
Nutritional info per serving:

Calories: 338
Fat: 26.4g
Net Carbs: 6.6g
Protein: 29.2g

Ingredients:

- 1 pound pork loin, trimmed and cut into about 1-inch cubes
- 2 tablespoons Spanish paprika, divided
- Salt and ground black pepper, as required
- 3 tablespoons butter, divided
- 12 ounces fresh white mushrooms, cut into thick slices
- 1 yellow onion, finely chopped
- 1 teaspoon garlic, finely minced
- ½ teaspoon dried thyme
- 1 (14½-ounces) can petite diced tomatoes with juice
- ½ cup homemade chicken broth
- 2/3 cup heavy cream
- 1 tablespoon fresh lemon juice

Instructions:

1. In a bowl, add the pork cubes, 1 tablespoon of paprika, salt, and black pepper and toss to coat well.
2. In a heavy wok, melt 1 tablespoon of butter over medium-high heat and sear the pork cubes for about 5-6 minutes.
3. With a slotted spoon, transfer the pork cubes onto a plate.
4. In the same wok, melt 1 tablespoon of butter over medium heat and cook the mushrooms for about 5 minutes.
5. With a slotted spoon, transfer the mushrooms onto a plate.
6. In the same wok again, melt the remaining butter over medium heat and sauté the onion for about 3-5 minutes.
7. Add the garlic, thyme, and remaining paprika and sauté for about 1-2 minutes.
8. Add the tomatoes with juice, and broth and bring to a boil.
9. Cook for about 10 minutes or until the mixture becomes slightly thick.
10. Stir in the cooked pork cubes, and mushrooms and simmer, covered for about 10 minutes.
11. Remove the wok from heat and immediately, stir in the cream, lemon juice, salt, and black pepper.
12. Serve hot.

Baked Pork Sausage with Vegetables:

Serves: 2 | Ready in about: 50 minutes
Nutritional info per serving:

Calories: 411
Fat: 32g
Net Carbs: 6.5g
Protein: 14.7g

Ingredients:

- 1 tablespoon olive oil
- ½ pound pork sausages
- 2 tomatoes, chopped
- 1 small onion, sliced
- ½ medium carrot, sliced
- 1 teaspoon smoked paprika
- 1 red bell peppers, sliced
- 1 sprig rosemary, chopped
- 1 garlic clove, minced
- 1 tablespoon balsamic vinegar
- Salt and black pepper to taste

Instructions:

1. Preheat the oven to 360° F.
2. Heat olive oil in a casserole and add the tomatoes, bell peppers, garlic, carrot, onion, and balsamic vinegar, and cook for 8-10 minutes until softened and lightly golden. Season with salt, smoked paprika, and black pepper.
3. Arrange the sausages on top of the veggies. Put the pan in the oven and bake for 20-25 minutes until the sausages have browned to the desired color. Serve sprinkled with rosemary.

Pork Osso Bucco:

Serves: 6 | Ready in about: 1 hour 55 minutes

Nutritional info per serving:

Calories: 590
Fat: 40g
Net Carbs: 6.1g
Protein: 34g

Ingredients:

- 4 tablespoons butter, softened
- 6 (16 oz) pork shanks
- 2 tablespoons vegetable oil
- 3 cloves garlic, minced
- 1 cup diced tomatoes
- Salt and black pepper to taste
- ½ cup chopped onions
- ½ cup chopped celery
- ½ cup chopped carrots
- 2 cups Cabernet
- 5 cups vegetable broth
- ½ cup chopped parsley + extra to garnish
- 2 teaspoons lemon peel

Instructions:

1. Melt the butter during a large saucepan over medium heat. Season the pork with salt and black pepper and brown it for 12 minutes; remove to a plate.
2. In the same pan, sauté 2 cloves of garlic and onions within the oil, for 3 minutes; return the pork shanks.
3. Stir within the Cabernet, carrots, celery, tomatoes, and vegetable broth; season with salt and pepper.
4. Cover the pan and let simmer on low heat for 1 ½ hour basting the pork every quarter-hour with the sauce.
5. In a bowl, mix the remaining garlic, parsley, and lemon peel to form a gremolata, and stir the mixture into the sauce when it's ready.
6. Turn the warmth off and dish the Osso Bucco. Garnish with parsley and serve with creamy turnip mash.

Fried Pork & Cilantro:

Serves: 4 | Ready in about: 30 minutes
Nutritional info per serving:

Calories: 343
Fat: 21.7g
Net Carbs: 5.6g
Protein: 30.7g

Ingredients

- 1 pound tender pork, trimmed and thinly sliced
- 1 tablespoon fresh ginger, finely chopped
- 4 garlic cloves, finely chopped
- 1 cup fresh cilantro, chopped and divided
- ¼ cup plus 1 tablespoon olive oil, divided
- 1 yellow onion, thinly sliced
- 1 large green bell pepper
- seeded and thinly sliced
- 1 tablespoon fresh lime juice
- Salt and ground black pepper, as required

Instructions

1. In a large bowl, mix well pork, ginger, garlic, ½ cup of cilantro, and ¼ cup of oil.
2. Refrigerate to marinate for about 2 hours.
3. Heat a large wok over medium-high heat and stir fry the pork with marinade for about 4-5 minutes.
4. Transfer the pork into a bowl.
5. In the same wok, heat the remaining oil over medium heat and sauté the onion for about 3-4 minutes.
6. Stir in the bell pepper and stir fry for about 3-4 minutes.
7. Stir in the cooked pork, lime juice, remaining cilantro, salt, and black pepper and cook for about 2 minutes.
8. Remove from the heat and serve hot.

Pork Steaks with Carrot & Broccoli:

Serves: 2 | Ready in about: 40 minutes
Nutritional info per serving:

Calories: 674
Fat: 46g
Net Carbs: 7.5g
Protein: 51.4g

Ingredients:

- 1 tablespoon olive oil
- 1 tablespoon butter
- 2 pork steaks, bone-in
- ½ cup water
- Salt and black pepper, to taste
- 2 garlic cloves, minced
- 1 tablespoon fresh parsley, chopped
- ½ head broccoli, cut into florets
- 1 carrot, sliced
- ½ lemon, sliced

Instructions:

1. Heat oil and butter over high heat. Add in the pork steaks, season with pepper and salt, and cook until browned; set to a plate. In the same pan, add garlic, carrot and broccoli and cook for 4 minutes.
2. Pour the water, lemon slices, salt, and black pepper, and cook everything for 5 minutes.
3. Return the pork steaks to the pan and cook for 10 minutes. Serve the steaks sprinkled with sauce with parsley.

Pork Nachos:

Serves: 4 | Ready in about: 15 minutes
Nutritional info per serving:

Calories: 452
Fat: 25g
Net Carbs: 9.3g
Protein: 22g

Ingredients:

- 1 bag low carb tortilla chips
- 2 cups leftover pulled pork
- 1 red bell pepper, seeded and chopped
- 1 red onion, diced
- 2 cups shredded Monterey Jack cheese

Instructions:

1. Preheat oven to 350°F.
2. Arrange the chips in a medium cast-iron pan, scatter pork over, followed by red bell pepper, and onion, and sprinkle with cheese.
3. Place the pan in the oven and cook for 10 minutes until the cheese has melted.
4. Allow cooling for 3 minutes and serve.

Pork with Brussels Sprout:

Serves: 5 | Ready in about: 25 minutes
Nutritional info per serving:

Calories: 348
Fat: 14.4g
Net Carbs: 7.1g
Protein: 44.2g

Ingredients:

- 3 tablespoons butter
- 1 1/3 pounds pork belly, cut into bite-sized pieces
- 1 pound fresh Brussels sprouts,
- trimmed and halved
- 2 garlic cloves, minced
- 2 tablespoons low-sodium soy sauce
- 1 tablespoon balsamic vinegar
- Ground black pepper, as required
- 1 scallion, sliced

Instructions:

1. Melt the butter in a large wok over medium-high heat and cook the pork pieces for about 3-4 minutes or until golden brown.
2. Stir in the Brussels sprouts and garlic and stir fry for about 3-4 minutes.
3. Add the soy sauce, vinegar, and black pepper and cook for about 1-2 minutes.
4. Stir in the scallion and serve hot.

Roasted Pork Stuffed with Ham & Cheese:

Serves: 2 | Ready in about: 40 minutes
Nutritional info per serving:

Calories: 433
Fat: 38.3g
Net Carbs: 4.2g
Protein: 24.3g

Ingredients:

- 2 tablespoons olive oil
- Zest and juice from 1 lime
- 1 garlic clove, minced
- 2 tablespoons fresh cilantro, chopped
- 2 tablespoons fresh mint, chopped
- Salt and black pepper, to taste
- 1 teaspoon cumin
- 2 pork loin steaks
- 1 pickle, chopped
- 2 oz smoked ham, sliced
- 2 oz Gruyere cheese sliced
- 1 tablespoon mustard

Instructions:

1. Start with making the marinade: combine the lime zest, oil, black pepper, cumin, cilantro, lime juice, garlic, mint and salt, in a food processor.
2. Place the steaks in the marinade, and toss well to coat; set aside for some hours in the fridge.
3. Arrange the steaks on a working surface, split the pickles, mustard, cheese, and ham on them, roll, and secure with toothpicks.
4. Heat a pan over medium heat, add in the pork rolls, cook each side for 2 minutes and remove to a baking sheet. Bake in the oven at 350^0 F for 25 minutes.

Garlicky Pork with Bell Peppers:

Serves: 4 | Ready in about: 40 minutes
Nutritional info per serving:

Calories: 456
Fat: 25g
Net Carbs: 6g
Protein: 40g

Ingredients:

- 3 tablespoons butter
- 4 pork steaks, bone-in
- 1 cup chicken stock
- Salt and black pepper, to taste
- A pinch of lemon pepper
- 3 tablespoons olive oil
- 6 garlic cloves, minced
- 2 tablespoons fresh parsley, chopped
- 4 bell peppers, sliced
- 1 lemon, sliced

Instructions:

1. Heat a pan with 2 tablespoons oil and 2 tablespoons butter over medium heat.
2. Add in the pork steaks, season with black pepper and salt, and cook until browned; remove to a plate.
3. In the same pan, warm the rest of the oil and butter, add garlic and bell peppers and cook for 4 minutes.
4. Pour the chicken stock, lemon slices, salt, lemon pepper, and black pepper, and cook everything for 5 minutes.
5. Return the pork steaks to the pan and cook for 10 minutes.
6. Split the sauce and steaks among plates and sprinkle with parsley to serve.

Pork Liver with Scallion:

Serves: 3 | Ready in about: 21 minutes
Nutritional info per serving:

Calories: 273
Fat: 13.9g
Net Carbs: 7.1g
Protein: 29g

Ingredients:

- ½ teaspoon fresh ginger, grated
- ¼ teaspoon garlic, minced
- 3 tablespoons soy sauce
- 1 tablespoon red boat fish sauce
- 1 tablespoon fresh lemon juice
- 1 teaspoon Erythritol
- Ground black pepper, as required
- 10½ ounces pork liver, cut into ¼-inch slices
- 2 tablespoons olive oil
- 10 scallions, cut into two-inch lengths

Instructions:

1. In a bowl, mix well ginger, garlic, soy sauce, fish sauce, lemon juice, Erythritol, and black pepper.
2. Add the liver slices and generously coat with the mixture.
3. Cover the bowl and refrigerate to marinate for at least 2 hours.
4. Remove the liver slices from bowl, reserving the marinade.
5. In a large wok, heat the oil and cook liver slices for about 2 minutes, without stirring.
6. Flip and cook for about 1 more minute.
7. Add half of the scallions and reserved marinade and stir fry for about 1-2 minutes.
8. Stir in the remaining scallions and remove from the heat
9. Serve hot.

Mushroom Pork Chops with Steamed Broccoli:

Serves: 2 | Ready in about: 1 hour and 15 minutes

Nutritional info per serving:

Calories: 412
Fat: 31g
Net Carbs: 7.2g
Protein: 20.3g

Ingredients:

- 1 shallot, chopped
- 2 (10.5-ounce) can mushroom soup
- 2 pork chops
- ½ cup sliced mushrooms
- Salt and black pepper, to taste
- 1 tablespoon parsley
- ½ head broccoli, cut into florets

Instructions:

1. Steam the broccoli in salted water over medium heat for 6-8 minutes until tender. Set aside.
2. Preheat the oven to 370° F.
3. Season the pork chops with salt and pepper, and place in a greased baking dish.
4. Combine the mushroom soup, mushrooms, and onion, in a bowl.
5. Pour this mixture over the pork chops. Bake for 45 minutes. Sprinkle with parsley and serve with broccoli.

FISH & SEAFOOD

Crispy Salmon with Broccoli & Red Bell Pepper:

Serves: 2 | Ready in about: 30 minutes
Nutritional info per serving:

Calories: 563
Fat: 37g
Net Carbs: 6g
Protein: 54g

Ingredients:

- 2 salmon fillets
- Salt and black pepper to taste
- 2 tablespoons mayonnaise
- 2 tablespoons fennel seeds, crushed
- ½ head broccoli, cut in florets
- 1 red bell pepper, sliced
- 1 tablespoon olive oil
- 2 lemon wedges

Instructions:

1. Brush the salmon with mayonnaise and season with salt and black pepper.
2. Coat with fennel seeds, place in a lined baking dish and bake for 15 minutes at 3700 F.
3. Steam the broccoli and carrot for 3-4 minutes, or until tender, in a pot over medium heat.
4. Heat the olive oil in a saucepan and sauté the red bell pepper for 5 minutes.
5. Stir in the broccoli and turn off the heat. Let the pan sit on the warm burner for 2-3 minutes.
6. Serve with baked salmon garnished with lemon wedges.

SHRIMP AND BLACK BEAN ENCHILADAS:

Serves: 4 | Ready in about: 20 minutes
Nutritional info per serving:

Calories: 196
Fat: 12g
Net Carbs: 4g
Protein: 17g

Ingredients:

- 2 cans (10 g) of red or green enchilada sauce
- 1 lb. shrimp
- 2 cans (15 oz.) black beans
- 2 cups grated Mexican cheese mixture
- 12 to 13 small flour tortillas

Instructions:

1. Preheat the oven to 400° F. Put ¼ cup sauce (enchiladas) in a saucepan. Increase the heat and add the shrimp. Cook until the shrimp are clean and no longer transparent for about 5 minutes. Remove from the heated container.
2. Place the enchiladas in a 9 x 13-inch baking dish. Organize a pea breakfast, 3 or 4 shrimp, and a slice of cheese on an omelet. Fold the edges of the tortilla into the oven dish on the filling and with the seam facing down.
3. Repeat with the remaining tortillas. Pour out the rest of the enchilada sauce after preparing all the enchiladas.
4. Bake until all the cheese has melted for 15 minutes.

Tuna Steaks with Shirataki Noodles:

Serves: 4 | Ready in about: 30 minutes
Nutritional info per serving:

Calories: 310
Fat: 18.2g
Net Carbs: 2g
Protein: 22g

Ingredients:

- 1 pack (7 oz.) miracle noodle angel hair
- 3 cups of water
- 1 red bell pepper, seeded and halved
- 4 tuna steaks
- Salt and black pepper to taste
- Olive oil for brushing
- 2 tablespoons pickled ginger
- 2 tablespoons chopped cilantro

Instructions:

1. Cook the shirataki rice as per package instructions: In a colander, rinse the shirataki noodles with running cold water.
2. Bring a pot of salted water to a boil; blanch the noodles for 2 minutes.
3. Drain and transfer to a dry skillet over medium heat.
4. Dry roast for a minute until opaque.
5. Grease a grill's grate with cooking spray and preheat on medium heat. Season the red bell pepper and tuna with salt and black pepper, brush with olive oil, and grill covered.
6. Cook both for 3 minutes on each side. Transfer to a plate to cool. Dice bell pepper with a knife.
7. Assemble the noodles, tuna, and bell pepper in serving plate.
8. Top with pickled ginger and garnish with cilantro.
9. Serve with roasted sesame sauce.

Cod in Butter Sauce:

Serves: 2 | Ready in about: 28 minutes
Nutritional info per serving:

Calories: 301
Fat: 18.9g
Net Carbs: 2.2g
Protein: 31.1g

Ingredients:

- 2 (6-ounces) cod fillets
- 1 teaspoon onion powder
- Salt and ground black pepper, as required
- 3 tablespoons butter, divided
- 2 garlic cloves, minced
- 1-2 lemon slices
- 2 teaspoons fresh dill weed

Instructions:

1. Season each cod fillet evenly with the onion powder, salt, and black pepper.
2. Melt 1 tablespoon of butter in a medium skillet over high heat and cook the cod fillets for about 4-5 minutes per side.
3. Transfer the cod fillets onto a plate.
4. Meanwhile, in a frying pan, melt the remaining butter over low heat and sauté the garlic and lemon slices for about 40-60 seconds.
5. Stir in the cooked cod fillets and dill and cook, covered for about 1-2 minutes.
6. Remove the cod fillets from heat and transfer onto the serving plates.
7. Top with the pan sauce and serve immediately.

Sardines with Green Pasta & Sun-Dried Tomatoes:

Serves: 2 | Ready in about: 20 minutes
Nutritional info per serving:

Calories: 431
Fat: 28.3g
Net Carbs: 5.6g
Protein: 32.5g

Ingredients:

- 2 tablespoons olive oil
- 4 cups zoodles (spiraled zucchini)
- ½ pound whole fresh sardines gutted and cleaned
- ½ cup sun-dried tomatoes, drained and chopped
- 1 tablespoon dill
- 1 garlic clove, minced

Instructions:

1. Preheat the oven to 350° F and line a baking sheet with parchment paper.
2. Arrange the sardines on the dish, drizzle with olive oil, sprinkle with salt and black pepper. Bake in the oven for 10 minutes until the skin is crispy.
3. Warm oil in a skillet over medium heat and stir-fry the zucchini, garlic and tomatoes for 5 minutes.
4. Adjust the seasoning. Transfer the sardines to a plate and serve with the veggie pasta.

TILAPIA WITH PARMESAN BARK:

Serves: 4 | Ready in about: 16 minutes
Nutritional info per serving:

Calories: 210
Fat: 9.3g
Net Carbs: 1.3g
Protein: 28.9g

Ingredients:

- ¾ cup freshly grated Parmesan cheese
- 2 teaspoons pepper
- 1 tablespoon chopped parsley
- 4 tilapia fillets (4 us)
- Lemon cut into pieces

Instructions:

1. Preheat the oven to 400° F. Mix cheese in a shallow dish with pepper and parsley and season with salt and pepper.
2. Mix the fish in the cheese with olive oil and flirt. Place on a baking sheet with foil and bake for 10 to 12 minutes until the fish in the thickest part is opaque.
3. Serve the lemon slices with the fish.

Blackened Fish Tacos with Slaw:

Serves: 4 | Ready in about: 20 minutes
Nutritional info per serving:

Calories: 268
Fat: 20g
Net Carbs: 3.5g
Protein: 13.8g

Ingredients:

- 1 tablespoon olive oil
- 1 teaspoon chili powder
- 2 tilapia fillets
- 1 teaspoon paprika
- 4 low carb tortillas

Slaw:
- ½ cup red cabbage, shredded
- 1 tablespoon lemon juice
- 1 teaspoon apple cider vinegar
- 1 tablespoon olive oil
- Salt and black pepper to taste

Instructions:

1. Season the tilapia with chili powder and paprika. Heat the vegetable oil during a skillet over medium heat.
2. Add tilapia and cook until blackened, about 3 minutes per side. Cut into strips. Divide the tilapia between the tortillas. Combine all slaw ingredients in a bowl and top the fish to serve.

Parmesan Halibut:

Serves: 2 |Ready in about: 34 minutes
Nutritional info per serving:

Calories: 250
Fat: 9g
Net Carbs: 1.5g
Protein: 38.6g

Ingredients:

- 2 (6-ounces) halibut fillets
- Salt and ground black pepper, as required
- 3 tablespoons sour cream
- ¼ teaspoon dill weed
- ¼ teaspoon garlic powder [when will this be used?]
- 2 tablespoons Parmesan cheese, grated
- 3 tablespoons scallions, chopped and divided

Instructions:

1. Preheat the oven to 375⁰ F and line a medium baking sheet with parchment paper.
2. Season each halibut fillet with salt and black pepper.
3. Add the sour cream, dill weed, and garlic powder in a bowl and mix until well combined.
4. Stir in the Parmesan cheese and 2 tablespoons of scallion.
5. Arrange the halibut fillets onto the prepared baking sheet and top each evenly with the Parmesan mixture.
6. Bake for about 24 minutes or until desired doneness.
7. Remove the halibut fillets from the oven and transfer onto the serving plates.
8. Top with the remaining scallions and serve immediately.

Fish Tacos with Slaw, Lemon and Cilantro:

Serves: 2 | Ready in about: 20 minutes
Nutritional info per serving:

Calories: 385
Fat: 26g
Net Carbs: 6.5g
Protein: 23.8g

Ingredients:

- 1 tablespoon olive oil
- 1 teaspoon chili powder
- 2 halibut fillets, skinless, sliced
- 2 low carb tortillas

Slaw:
- 2 tablespoons red cabbage, shredded
- 1 tablespoon lemon juice
- Salt to taste
- ½ tablespoon extra-virgin olive oil
- ½ carrot, shredded
- 1 tablespoon cilantro, chopped

Instructions:

1. Combine red cabbage with salt in a bowl; massage cabbage to tenderize.
2. Add in the remaining slaw ingredient, toss to coat and set aside.
3. Rub the halibut with olive oil, chili powder and paprika.
4. Heat a grill pan over medium heat. Add halibut and cook until lightly charred and cooked through, about 3 minutes per side.
5. Divide between the tortillas. Combine all slaw ingredients in a bowl.
6. Split the slaw among the tortillas.

MOZZARELLA FISH:

Serves: 6-8 | Ready in about: 20 minutes

Nutritional info per serving:

Calories: 156
Fat: 6g
Net Carbs: 5g
Protein: 8g

Ingredients:

- 2 lbs. of bone gold sole
- Salt and pepper to taste
- ½ teaspoon dried oregano
- 1 cup grated mozzarella cheese
- 1 large fresh tomato, sliced thinly

Instructions:

1. Excellent source of cooking the butter. Organize a single layer of trout. Add salt, pepper, and oregano.
2. Top with sliced cheese slices and tomatoes.
3. Cook, covered, for 10 to 15 minutes at 425°F.

Sushi Shrimp Rolls:

Serves: 5 | Ready in about: 10 minutes
Nutritional info per serving:

Calories: 216
Fat: 10g
Net Carbs: 1g
Protein: 18.7g

Ingredients:

- 2 cups cooked and chopped shrimp
- 1 tablespoon sriracha sauce
- ¼ cucumber, julienned
- 5 hand roll nori sheets
- ¼ cup mayonnaise

Instructions:

1. Combine shrimp, mayonnaise, cucumber and sriracha sauce in a bowl.
2. Layout a single nori sheet on a flat surface and spread about 1/5 of the shrimp mixture.
3. Roll the nori sheet as desired. Repeat with the other ingredients.
4. Serve with sugar-free soy sauce.

Lemony Trout:

Serves: 6 | Ready in about: 40 minutes
Nutritional info per serving:

Calories: 469
Fat: 23.1g
Net Carbs: 0.7g
Protein: 60.7g

Ingredients:

- 2 (1½-pounds) wild-caught trout, gutted and cleaned
- Salt and ground black pepper, as required
- 1 lemon, sliced
- 2 tablespoons fresh dill, minced
- 2 tablespoons butter, melted
- 2 tablespoons fresh lemon juice

Instructions:

1. Preheat the oven to 475° F. Arrange a wire rack onto a foil-lined baking sheet.
2. Sprinkle the trout with salt and black pepper from inside and outside generously.
3. Fill the fish cavity with lemon slices and dill.
4. Place the trout onto the prepared baking sheet and drizzle with the melted butter and lemon juice.
5. Bake for about 25 minutes.
6. Remove the baking sheet from the oven and transfer the trout onto a serving platter.
7. Serve hot.

Prawns in Creamy Mushroom Sauce:

Serves: 2 | Ready in about: 35 minutes
Nutritional info per serving:

Calories: 772
Fat: 59.7g
Net Carbs: 6.4g
Protein: 50.7g

Ingredients:

- 8 ounces prawns, peeled and deveined
- 1¼ cups fresh mushrooms, sliced
- 4 bacon slices, cut into 1-inch pieces
- 1½ cups heavy whipping cream
- 1 jalapeño pepper, chopped
- 1 teaspoon fresh thyme, chopped
- Salt and ground black pepper, as required

Instructions:

1. Heat a skillet over medium heat and cook the bacon for about 5 minutes, stirring frequently.
2. Add the mushrooms and cook for about 5-6 minutes, stirring frequently.
3. Add the prawns and stir to combine.
4. Increase the heat to high and stir fry for about 2 minutes.
5. Add the cream, jalapeño pepper, thyme, salt, and black pepper and stir to combine.
6. Lower the heat to medium and cook for about 1 more minute.
7. Remove the skillet from heat and serve hot.

VEGGIES & SIDES

Tofu & Vegetable Stir-Fry:

Serves: 2 | Ready in about: 10 minutes
Nutritional info per serving:

Calories: 423
Fat: 31g
Net Carbs: 7.3g
Protein: 25.5g

Ingredients:

- 2 tablespoons olive oil
- 1 ½ cups extra-firm tofu, pressed and cubed
- 1 ½ tablespoons flaxseed meal
- Salt and black pepper, to taste
- 1 garlic clove, minced
- 1 tablespoon soy sauce, sugar-free
- ½ head broccoli, break into florets
- 1 teaspoon onion powder
- 1 cup mushrooms, sliced
- 1 tablespoon sesame seeds

Instructions:

1. In a bowl, add onion powder, tofu, salt, soy sauce, black pepper, flaxseed, and garlic. Toss the mixture to coat and allow marinating for 20-30 minutes.
2. In a pan, warm oil over medium heat, add in broccoli, mushrooms and tofu mixture and stir-fry for 6-8 minutes.
3. Serve sprinkled with sesame seeds.

KETO PEANUT BUTTER RAMEN:

Serves: 1 | Ready in about: 10 minutes
Nutritional info per serving:

Calories: 574
Fat: 49g
Net Carbs: 13.5g
Protein: 23g

Ingredients:

- Sweet and spicy peanut sauce
- ¼ cup all-natural peanut butter (no added sugar, crisp or fresh)
- 1 teaspoon sambal oelek (add more if you like spicy)
- 1 ½ tablespoons soy sauce
- 1 teaspoon Trivia or another sugar-free sweetener that you like

Noodles and toppings

- 1 pack of House Foods Shirataki noodles
- 1 block of extra healthy tofu (about 100 g)
- 1 tablespoons coconut oil
- 1-2 chopped green onions
- 1 chopped cayenne pepper
- Sesame seed drizzle (optional)

Instructions:

1. Cut the tofu into large cubes and heat frying pan over medium heat.
2. Add the coconut oil (1 tablespoon) and add it to the tofu. Stir so that the tofu does not stick.
3. Once the tofu starts to turn a bit brown, turn it on with more soy sauce and stir. Remove the fire and reserve.
4. You want the tofu to have a crispy exterior, but a sweet center.
5. Boil water (2 cups are enough). While the water boils, put the peanut butter (4 tablespoons) in a large bowl with the sambal oelek (chili paste), soy sauce (1 tablespoon) and the Truvia (1 teaspoon).
6. Slowly add ⅓ cup boiled water into the large bowl. Mix well to emulsify. Depending on how you are, you may need a little more hot water or less. You are looking for a sauce that is neither thick nor liquid.
7. Remove the noodles from the package and place it in the microwave for 2 minutes add the noodles to the peanut sauce and mix. When combined, sesame seeds, soy sauce, and chopped cayenne pepper.

Cauliflower Gouda Casserole:

Serves: 4 | Ready in about: 21 minutes
Nutritional info per serving:

Calories: 215
Fat: 15g
Net Carbs: 4g
Protein: 12g

Ingredients:

- 2 heads cauliflower, cut into florets
- ⅓ Cup butter, cubed
- 2 tablespoons melted butter
- 1 white onion, chopped
- Salt and black pepper to taste
- ¼ almond milk
- ½ cup almond flour
- 1 ½ cups grated Gouda cheese

Instructions:

1. Preheat oven to 350°F and put the cauli florets in a large microwave-safe bowl.
2. Sprinkle with a bit of water, and steam in the microwave for 4 to 5 minutes.
3. Melt the ⅓ cup of butter in a saucepan over medium heat and sauté the onion for 3 minutes.
4. Add the cauliflower, season with salt and black pepper and mix in almond milk. Simmer for 3 minutes.
5. Mix the remaining melted butter with almond flour. Stir into the cauliflower as well as half of the cheese.
6. Sprinkle the top with the remaining cheese and bake for 10 minutes until the cheese has melted and golden brown on the top.
7. Plate the bake and serve with salad.

Cabbage Casserole:

Serves: 3 | Ready in about: 45 minutes
Nutritional info per serving:

Calories: 273
Fat: 24.8g
Net Carbs: 5.6g
Protein: 6.2g

Ingredients:

- ½ head cabbage
- 2 scallions, chopped
- 4 tablespoons unsalted butter
- 2 ounces cream cheese, softened
- ¼ cup Parmesan cheese, grated
- ¼ cup fresh cream
- ½ teaspoon Dijon mustard
- 2 tablespoons fresh parsley, chopped
- Salt and ground black pepper, as required

Instructions:

1. Preheat the oven to 350°F.
2. Cut the cabbage head in half, lengthwise. Then cut into 4 equal-sized wedges.
3. In a pan of boiling water, add the cabbage wedges and cook, covered for about 5 minutes.
4. Drain the cabbage well.
5. Now, arrange the cabbage wedges into a small baking dish.
6. Melt the butter in a small pan and sauté the scallions for about 5 minutes.
7. Add the remaining ingredients and stir to combine.
8. Remove from heat and immediately, place the cheese mixture over cabbage wedges.
9. Bake for about 20 minutes.
10. Remove the baking dish of cabbage mixture from the oven and let it cool for about 5 minutes before serving.
11. Cut into 3 equal-sized portions and serve.

Mediterranean Eggplant Squash Pasta:

Serves: 2 | Ready in about: 15 minutes
Nutritional info per serving:

Calories: 388
Fat: 17.8g
Net Carbs: 9.6g
Protein: 12g

Ingredients:

- 2 tablespoons butter
- 1 cup cherry tomatoes
- 2 tablespoons parsley, chopped
- 1 eggplant, cubed
- ¼ cup Parmesan cheese
- 3 tablespoons scallions, chopped
- 1 cup green beans
- 1 teaspoon lemon zest
- 10 oz. butternut squash, spirals

Instructions:

1. In a saucepan over medium heat, add the butter to melt.
2. Cook the spaghetti squash for 4-5 minutes and remove to a plate.
3. In the same saucepan, cook eggplant for 5 minutes until tender.
4. Add the tomatoes and green beans, and cook for 5 more minutes.
5. Stir in parsley, zest, and scallions, and remove the pan from heat.
6. Stir in spaghetti squash and Parmesan cheese to serve.

SIMPLE VEGAN BOK CHOY SOUP:

Serves: 1 | Ready in about: 5 minutes

Nutritional info per serving:

Calories: 92
Fat: 0.3g
Net Carbs: 4g
Protein: 2g

Ingredients:

- 2 chopped bok Choy stalks
- 1 cup vegetable broth
- 1 teaspoon nutritional yeast
- 2 dashes of garlic powder
- 2 pinches of onion powder
- salt and pepper to taste

Instructions:

1. Mix all ingredients in a bowl and mix.
2. Microwave for 3 min

Creamy Vegetable Stew:

Serves: 4 | Ready in about: 32 minutes

Nutritional info per serving:

Calories: 310
Fat: 26.4g
Net Carbs: 6g
Protein: 8g

Ingredients:

- 2 tablespoons ghee
- 1 tablespoon onion-garlic puree
- 4 medium carrots, chopped
- 1 large head cauliflower, cut into florets
- 2 cups green beans, halved
- Salt and black pepper to taste
- 1 cup water
- 1 ½ cups heavy cream

Instructions:

1. Melt ghee in a saucepan over medium heat and sauté onion-garlic puree to be fragrant, 2 minutes.
2. Stir in carrots, cauliflower, and green beans, salt, and black pepper, add the water, stir again, and cook the vegetables on low heat for 25 minutes to soften.
3. Mix in the heavy cream to be incorporated, turn the heat off, and adjust the taste with salt and pepper.
4. Serve the stew with almond flour bread.

Broccoli Mash:

Serves: 6 |Ready in about: 20 minutes
Nutritional info per serving:

Calories: 32
Fat: 0.9g
Net Carbs: 3.1g
Protein: 2g

Ingredients:

- 16 ounces broccoli florets
- 1 cup of water
- 1 teaspoon fresh lemon juice
- 1 teaspoon butter, softened
- 1 teaspoon garlic, minced
- Salt and ground black pepper, as required

1. In a medium pan, add the broccoli and water over medium heat and cook for about 5 minutes.
2. Drain the broccoli well and transfer into a large bowl.
3. In the bowl of broccoli, add the lemon juice, butter, and garlic and with an immersion blender blend until smooth.
4. Season with salt and black pepper and serve.

Roasted Brussels Sprouts & Bacon:

Serves: 2-4 |Ready in about: 40 minutes
Nutritional info per serving:

Calories: 183
Fat: 15.6g
Net Carbs: 1.5g
Protein: 8.8g

Ingredients:

- 1 tablespoons olive oil
- 1 garlic clove, sliced
- 6 pearl onions, halved
- 3 tablespoons vinegar
- 1 tablespoon erythritol
- Salt and black pepper to taste
- 1 lb. Brussels sprouts, halved
- 4 oz. bacon, chopped

Instructions:

1. Preheat oven to 400⁰ F and line a baking sheet with parchment paper.
2. Mix balsamic, erythritol, olive oil, salt, and black pepper and combine with the Brussels sprouts, garlic, bacon, and pearl onions, in a bowl.
3. Spread the mixture on the baking sheet and roast for 30 minutes until tender on the inside and crispy on the outside. Serve immediately.

KETO CAULIFLOWER HASH BROWNS:

Serves: 4 | Ready in about: 40 minutes
Nutritional info per serving:

Calories: 282
Fat: 26g
Net Carbs: 5g
Protein: 7g

Ingredients:

- 1 lb. cauliflower
- 3 eggs
- ½ yellow onion, grated
- 1 teaspoon salt
- 2 pinches pepper
- 4 oz. butter, for frying

Instructions:

1. Use a food processor or grater to clean, cut, and grate the cauliflower.
2. Add a large bowl of cauliflower. Remove the rest of the ingredients and blend. Set 5–10 minutes aside.
3. Melt a generous quantity of butter or oil in a large skillet over medium heat. When you intend to have space for 3–4 pancakes (approximately 3–4 inches each) at a time, the cooking process will go faster.
4. Use the low heat oven to keep the pancakes first lots hot while you're making the others.
5. Place the rubbed cauliflower scoops in the frying pan and carefully flatten them until they are about 3–4 inches in diameter.
6. Fry on both sides for 4–5 minutes to make sure they don't burn, adjust the heat.

Zucchini Gratin with Feta Cheese:

Serves: 6 | Ready in about: 65 minutes
Nutritional info per serving:

Calories: 264
Fat: 21g
Net Carbs: 4g
Protein: 14g

Ingredients:

- 2 lb. zucchinis, sliced
- 2 red bell peppers, seeded and sliced
- Salt and black pepper to taste
- 1 ½ cups crumbled feta cheese
- 2 tablespoons butter, melted
- ¼ teaspoon xanthan gum
- ½ cup heavy light whipping cream

Instructions:

1. Preheat oven to 370°F. Place the sliced zucchinis during a colander over the sink, sprinkle with salt and let sit for 20 minutes.
2. Transfer to paper towels to empty the surplus liquid.
3. Grease a baking dish with cooking spray and make a layer of zucchini and bell peppers overlapping each other.
4. Season with pepper, and sprinkle with feta cheese. Repeat the layering process a second time.
5. Combine the butter, xanthan gum, and light whipping cream during a bowl, stir to combine completely and pour over the vegetables.
6. Bake for 30-40 minutes
7. Or until golden brown on top.

Spiced mushroom:

Serves: 2 |Ready in about: 31 minutes
Nutritional info per serving:

Calories: 154
Fat: 12.2g
Net Carbs: 7g
Protein: 4.6g

Ingredients:

- 2 tablespoons butter
- ½ teaspoon cumin seeds, lightly crushed
- 1 yellow onion, thinly sliced
- ½ pound white button mushrooms, chopped
- 1 green chili, chopped
- 1 teaspoon ground coriander
- ½ teaspoon graham masala powder
- ½ teaspoon red chili powder
- 1/8 teaspoon ground turmeric
- Salt, as required
- 2 tablespoons fresh cilantro leaves, chopped

Instructions:

1. Melt the butter in a skillet over medium heat and sauté the cumin seeds for about 1 minute.
2. Add the onion and sauté for about 4-5 minutes.
3. Add the mushrooms and sauté for about 5-7 minutes.
4. Add the green chili, spices, and salt and sauté for about 1-2 minutes.
5. Stir in the cilantro and sauté for about 1 more minute.
6. Serve hot.

Roasted Green Beans with Garlic & Almond Flakes:

Serves: 2-4 | Ready in about: 30 minutes
Nutritional info per serving:

Calories: 187
Fat: 12.3g
Net Carbs: 4.5g
Protein: 3.5g

Ingredients:

- 2 tablespoons butter, melted
- ¼ cup almond flakes
- ¼ cup pork rind crumbs
- 2 garlic cloves, sliced
- Salt and black pepper to taste
- 1 lb. green beans, thread removed

Instructions:

1. Preheat oven to 400⁰ F.
2. Place the green beans and garlic in a baking dish, and season with salt and black pepper.
3. Pour the butter over and toss to coat. Bake for 20 minutes.
4. In a dry pan over medium heat, toast the almonds until golden.
5. Pour over the green beans to serve.

DESSERTS & DRINKS

Coconut Panna Cotta with Cream & Caramel:

Serves: 2-4 | Ready in about: 10 minutes
Nutritional info per serving:

Calories: 268
Fat: 31g
Net Carbs: 2.5g
Protein: 6.5g

Ingredients:

- 4 eggs
- 1/3 cup erythritol, for caramel
- 2 cups of coconut milk
- 1 tablespoon vanilla extract
- 1 tablespoon lemon zest
- ½ cup erythritol, for custard
- 2 cup heavy whipping cream
- Mint leaves, to serve

Instructions:

1. In a deep pan, heat the erythritol for the caramel.
2. Add two tablespoons of water and bring to a boil. Lower the heat and cook until the caramel turns to a golden brown color.
3. Divide between 4 metal tins, set aside and let cool.
4. In a bowl, mix the eggs, remaining erythritol, lemon zest, and vanilla. Beat in the coconut milk until well combined.
5. Pour the custard into each caramel-lined ramekin and place them into a deep baking tin. Fill over the way with the remaining hot water. Bake at 350° F for around 45 minutes.
6. Carefully, take out the ramekins with tongs and refrigerate for at least 3 hours.
7. Run a knife slowly around the edges to invert onto a dish.
8. Serve with dollops of whipped cream and scattered with mint leaves.

Chocolate Marshmallows:

Serves: 4 |Ready in about: half-hour
Nutritional info per serving:

Calories: 55
Fat: 2.2g
Net Carbs: 5.1g
Protein: 0.5g

Ingredients:

- 2 tablespoons unsweetened chocolate
- ½ teaspoon vanilla
- ½ cup swerve
- 1 tablespoon xanthan gum mixed in 1 tablespoon water
- A pinch Salt
- 6 tablespoon cool water
- 2 ½ teaspoons gelatin powder

Dusting:
- 1 tablespoon unsweetened chocolate
- 1 tablespoon swerves confectioner's sugar

Instructions:

1. Line the loaf pan with parchment paper and grease with cooking spray; put aside.
2. In a saucepan, mix the swerve, 2 tablespoons of water, xanthan gum mixture, and salt.
3. Place the pan over medium heat and convey it to a boil. Insert the thermometer and let the ingredients simmer to 240°F, for 7 minutes.
4. In a small bowl, add 2 tablespoons of water and sprinkle the gelatin on top.
5. Let sit there without stirring to dissolve for five minutes.
6. While the gelatin dissolves, pour the remaining water during a small bowl and warmth within the microwave for 30 seconds. Stir in chocolate and blend it into the gelatin.
7. When the sugar solution has hit the proper temperature, gradually pour it directly into the gelatin mixture while continuously whisking.
8. Beat for 10 minutes to urge a light-weight and fluffy consistency.
9. Next, stir within the vanilla and pour the blend into the loaf pan. Let the marshmallows set for 3 hours then use an oiled knife to chop it into cubes; place them on a plate.
10. Mix the remaining chocolate and confectioner's sugar together. Sift it over the marshmallows.

Vanilla Crème Brûlée:

Serves: 4 | Ready in about: 1 hour 20 minutes
Nutritional info per serving:

Calories: 264
Fat: 26.7g
Net Carbs: 2.4g
Protein: 3.9g

Ingredients:

- 2 cups heavy cream
- 1 vanilla bean, halved and scraped out seeds
- 4 organic egg yolks
- 1/3 teaspoon stevia powder
- 1 teaspoon organic vanilla extract
- Pinch of salt
- 4 tablespoons granulated Erythritol

Instructions:

1. Preheat the oven to 350°F.
2. Place the heavy cream in a pan over medium heat and cook until heated.
3. Stir in the vanilla bean seeds and bring to a gentle boil.
4. Adjust the heat to very low and cook, covered for about 20 minutes.
5. Meanwhile, in a bowl, add the remaining ingredients except for Erythritol and beat until thick and pale mixture forms.
6. Remove the heavy cream from heat and through a fine-mesh strainer, strain into a heatproof bowl.
7. Slowly, add the cream in egg yolk mixture beating continuously until well combined.
8. Divide the mixture into 4 ramekins.
9. Arrange the ramekins into a large baking dish.
10. In the baking dish, add hot water about half of the ramekins.
11. Bake for about 30-35 minutes.
12. Remove the baking dish from the oven and let the ramekins cool slightly.
13. Refrigerate the ramekins for at least 4 hours.
14. Just before serving, sprinkle the ramekins evenly with Erythritol.
15. Holding a kitchen torch about 4-5-inch from the top, caramelize the Erythritol for about 2 minutes.
16. Set aside for 5 minutes before serving.

Healthy Chia Pudding with Strawberries:

Serves: 2 | Ready in about: 10 minutes
Nutritional info per serving:

Calories: 187
Fat: 11g
Net Carbs: 6.3g
Protein: 6.7g

Ingredients:

- 1 cup yogurt, full-fat
- 2 teaspoons xylitol
- 2 tablespoons chia seeds
- 1 cup fresh strawberries, sliced
- 1 tablespoon lemon zest
- Mint leaves, to serve

Instructions:

1. In a bowl, combine the yogurt and xylitol together.
2. Add in the chia seeds and stir. Reserve a couple of strawberries for garnish, and mash the remaining ones with a fork until pureed.
3. Stir in the yogurt mixture and refrigerate for 45 minutes.
4. Once cooled, divide the mixture between glasses.
5. Top each with the reserved slices of strawberries, mint leaves, and lemon zest.

Lemon Cheesecake Mousse:

Serves: 4 | Ready in about: 5 minutes
Nutritional info per serving:

Calories: 223
Fat: 18g
Net Carbs: 3g
Protein: 12g

Ingredients:

- 24 oz. cream cheese softened
- 2 cups swerve confectioner's sugar
- 2 lemons, juiced and zested
- Pink salt to taste
- 1 cup whipped cream + extra for garnish

Instructions:

1. Whip the cream cheese in a bowl with a hand mixer until light and fluffy.
2. Mix in the swerve sugar, lemon juice, and salt. Fold in the whipped cream to evenly combine.
3. Spoon the mousse into serving cups and refrigerate to thicken for 1 hour.
4. Swirl with extra whipped cream and garnish lightly with lemon zest. Serve immediately.

Chocolate Lava Cake:

Serves: 2 | Ready in about: 24 minutes

Nutritional info per serving:

Calories: 436
Fat: 25.2g
Net Carbs: 4.9g
Protein: 10.4g

Ingredients:

- 2 ounces 70% dark chocolate
- 2 ounces unsalted butter
- 2 organic eggs
- 2 tablespoons powdered Erythritol plus more for dusting
- 1 tablespoon almond flour
- 6 fresh raspberries

Instructions:

1. Preheat the oven to 350°F. Grease 2 ramekins.
2. In a microwave-safe bowl, add the chocolate, and butter and microwave on High for about 2 minutes or until melted, stirring after every 30 seconds.
3. Remove the bowl from microwave and stir until smooth.
4. Place the eggs in a bowl and with a wire whisk, beat well.
5. Add the chocolate mixture, Erythritol, and almond flour and mix until well combined.
6. Divide the mixture evenly into prepared ramekins.
7. Bake for about 9 minutes or until the top is set.
8. Remove the ramekins from the oven and set aside for about 1-2 minutes.
9. Carefully, invert the cakes onto serving plates and dust with extra powdered Erythritol.
10. Garnish with fresh raspberries and serve.

Almond Milk Berry Shake:

Serves: 2 | Ready in about: 5 minutes
Nutritional info per serving:

Calories: 228
Fat: 21g
Net Carbs: 5.4g
Protein: 7.9g

Ingredients:

- ½ cup fresh blueberries
- ½ cup raspberries
- ½ cup almond milk
- ¼ cup heavy cream
- Maple syrup to taste, sugar-free
- 1 tablespoon sesame seeds
- Chopped pistachios for topping
- 1 teaspoon chopped mint leaves

Instructions:

1. Combine the blueberries, milk, heavy cream, and syrup in a blender.
2. Process until smooth and pour into serving glasses.
3. Top with the sesame seeds, pistachios, and mint leaves.
4. Serve immediately.

Creamy Coconut Kiwi Drink:

Serves: 4 | Ready in about: 3 minutes
Nutritional info per serving:

Calories: 351
Fat: 28g
Net Carbs: 9.7g
Protein: 16g

Ingredients:

- 5 kiwis, pulp scooped
- 2 tablespoons erythritol
- 2 cups unsweetened coconut milk
- 2 cups coconut cream
- 7 ice cubes
- Mint leaves to garnish

Instructions:

1. In a blender, process the kiwis, erythritol, milk, cream, and ice cubes until smooth, about 3 minutes.
2. Pour into four serving glasses, garnish with mint leaves, and serve.

Butter Coffee:

Serves: 2 | Ready in about: 10 minutes
Nutritional info per serving:

Calories: 110
Fat: 12.6g
Net Carbs: 0g
Protein: 0.1g

Ingredients:

- 2 cups of water
- 2 tablespoons ground coffee
- 1 tablespoon coconut oil
- 1 tablespoon butter

Instructions:

1. In a pan, add the water and coffee over medium heat and cook for about 5 minutes.
2. Through a strainer, strain the coffee into a blender.
3. Add the coconut oil, and butter and pulse until light and creamy.
4. Transfer into two mugs and serve immediately.

Green Detox Drink:

Serves: 2 | Ready in about: 5 minutes
Nutritional info per serving:

Calories: 423
Fat: 34.2g
Net Carbs: 9.5g
Protein: 8.2g

Ingredients:

- 2 large ripe avocados, halved and pitted
- 1 small cucumber, peeled and chopped
- 2 tablespoons swerve sugar
- ¼ cup cold almond milk
- ½ teaspoon vanilla extract
- 1 tablespoon cold heavy cream

Instructions:

1. In a blender, add the avocado pulp, cucumber, swerve sugar, almond milk, vanilla extract, and heavy cream.
2. Process until smooth.
3. Pour the mixture into 2 tall serving glasses, garnish with strawberries, and serve immediately.

Ginger Lemonade:

Serves: 4 |Ready in about: 10 minutes
Nutritional info per serving:

Calories: 13
Fat: 0.3g
Net Carbs: 1.8g
Protein: 0.4g

Ingredients:

- 4-5 tablespoons fresh lemon juice
- 2 tablespoons fresh ginger, peeled and grated
- 1/3 cup powdered Erythritol
- 4 cups of water
- Ice cubes, as required

Instructions:

1. In a pitcher, add the lemon juice, ginger, Erythritol, and water and stir until sweetener is dissolved.
2. Fill 4 serving glasses with ice cubes and top with the lemonade.
3. Serve chilled.

Iced Coffee:

Serves: 2 |Ready in about: 10 minutes
Nutritional info per serving:

Calories: 118
Net Carbs: 0.8g
Protein: 0.6g
Fat: 12.6g

Ingredients:

- 2 cups chilled brewed coffee
- 2 tablespoons heavy cream
- 1 tablespoon MCT oil
- 1 cup ice cubes
- 1 teaspoon organic vanilla extract
- ½ teaspoon liquid stevia
- ¼ teaspoon xanthan gum
- ¼ teaspoon ground cinnamon
- Pinch of sea salt.

Instructions:

1. Place the coffee, heavy cream, MCT oil and 1 cup of ice cubes in a blender and pulse on high speed until well combined.
2. Add the remaining ingredients and pulse until smooth.
3. Add the desired amount of ice cubes into glasses.
4. Pour coffee over ice and serve.

CONCLUSION:

Thank you for reading this book and having the patience to try the recipes.

I do hope that you gain as much enjoyment reading and experimenting with the meals as I have had writing these books.

If you would like to leave a comment, you can do it at the Order section->Digital order send and also buy paperback, in your Amazon account.

Stay safe and healthy!

Printed in Great Britain
by Amazon